REALITY OF SPIRITUALITY IN KALYUG

BY
PULKIT MOHAN SINGLA
(HALL OF POETS)

EARTH VISION PUBLICATIONS
H-23/16, DLF Phase - I, Gurgaon-122002
Ph. : +91 124-4054392, 09811842292, 09034006808
e-mail: earthvisionpublications@gmail.com
Website : www.earthvisionpublications.com

REALITY OF SPIRITUALITY IN KALYUG

COPYRIGHT 2016 © PULKIT MOHAN SINGLA

Spiritual (Non- Fiction , English)

ISBN: 978-93-84922-21-4 (Paper Back)
Price: ₹ 390.00
US Dollar: $ 26 (Includes Shipping Charges)

DISCLAIMER

This book is designed to provide information on spirituality in general. This information is provided and sold with the knowledge that the publisher and author do not offer any legal or other professional advice. This book does not contain all information available on the subject. This book is not intended to offend the religious or moral sentiments of any community, religion, region, race, sex or linguistic groups or vilify any person dead or alive. Every effort has been made to make this book as accurate as possible. However, there may be typographical and or content errors. Therefore, this book should serve only as a general guide and not as the ultimate source of subject information. This book contains information that might be dated and is intended only to educate and entertain. The author and publisher shall have no liability or responsibility to any person or entity regarding any loss or damage incurred, or alleged to have incurred, directly or indirectly, by the information contained in this book.

Published by:
EARTH VISION PUBLICATIONS

H-23/16, DLF Phase-I, Gurgaon - 122 002 (Haryana), India
Phone : 0124-4054392, 098118-42292

Email : earthvisionpublications@gmail.com, mgwebguru@gmail.com

Website : www.earthvisionpublications.com

Typeset by : www.atozwebguru.com

Book Available at : www.globalfraternityofpoets.com, www.amazon.in www.flipkart.com

Distributor : Shashi Kant Sharma,
H.No. 91, New Model Town Extension, Hisar
Phone : +91-90340-06808, +91-85108-44492

Special thanks to my Father Sh. Yogesh Mohan Singla and my Mother Late Smt. Madhu Singla for their outstanding efforts and their teachings in the path of spirituality. They have been my first teacher and always guided me on the right path since childhood. I also acknowledge the efforts of my elder sister Dr. Prerna Singla who guided me from time to time and supported me in the making of this book.

Painting by PULKIT MOHAN SINGLA

FOREWORD

This book was not planned on the cards but was a compilation of my experience and ideology which my son followed. I can proudly admit that I am a spiritual and sentimental person but that does not mean that I have to be superstitious and old. My son never told me that he is writing this wonderful book on spirituality but yes he irritated me as well as surprised me many a time by asking unrealistic but logical questions which were as real as him and as incredible as God. Spirituality is such a huge topic which cannot be covered in one name or one book; it is such a divine creation that it forms its own definition when it comes out from any individual. I never asked my son that why is he inquisitive about God or his existence in the world, but he was always curious and that why he is different from other kids. The child who should ask me to get him bat and ball, asked me why we are born on Earth? And besides my countless answers would not satisfy him. This phase of questioning, answering, arguments, counter-arguments and quest for the Truth has been going on since years and in the process my son has been through every phase of life from the death of his mother in childhood to his struggles with mathematics and from his passion for artwork to his craziness for writing and along with all these, his keen interest in understanding the Creation and the Divine Creator. As this book came to me I was surprised and became emotional. I never expected Pulkit to go so far in his search for Spirituality and the true meaning of the same. When I saw the first page of Reality Of Spirituality In Kalyug, where I and his mother are shown with the acknowledgment quotes and dedication, I couldn't resist my tears. This was the moment which made me really proud as a father. No money and no luxury can compare the feeling of being a proud father and especially when you learn something from your child, being God in human form which is your child who teaches you the lesson of life. As my lips were reading the words of his thoughts and wisdom, tears were finding their way towards heaven. A feeling of blessing was in my hands in the shape of the book and no matter how many struggles I or my son faced in this life, this book was not less than a bible for me, which was in his own way telling me the reality of life. I will not ask you to read this book because my son has written this. I am asking you to read this book because a son has written this.

Yogesh Mohan Singla

PREFACE

Dear Reader,

    Thank you for choosing "Reality of spirituality in Kalyug". This book is not an effort of a few days but an effort of many years, keen observations and analysis of spiritual teachings and deep study of society and nature. At some point in time we wonder if we can really find God.

Reality of spirituality in kalyug is a book that determines the true meaning of spirituality. It raises doubt on the so called blind faith coming from historical times which has created uncomfortable lives for millions of people. We all are becoming so addicted to superstition and miracles that we don't want to see the real picture of the kalyug. We still believe in the acts of mythical times besides knowing that the world today is different from the world in Mythical times. The God who should be remembered for humanity is worshiped for materialistic things. We are blindly walking on the well established fake path laid down for us by today's spiritual mentors. In the era of urbanisation we have betrayed not only ourselves but our God too. Religion is used for politics and politics is played for God.

The world is running in the search for God, to worship, to love and also to gain material pleasures. But is our approach right? Are the teachings we follow right and authentic??? Is there any God at all??

This book will compel you to question the religion, the being, the nature and the self. The things we know and the things we believe are different from the things that exist as truth and in this book of mine you will have the chance to explore the same.

This book not only discloses the myths we are living with but also the wrong teachings which are taught to us by spiritual mentors. We are mind washed so deeply that we feel that every action will make us a sinner. The book showcases the true reality of spirituality in kalyug and will provoke you to question spirituality, reality and even yourself.

This book is dedicated to my family and all the readers of Real world. I express my heartfelt gratitude to my readers and friends who believed in me and have always encouraged me to write.

Pulkit Mohan Singla
www.pulkitmohansingla.com

INTRODUCTION

Kalyug is the term given to today's era. The word 'kalyug' denotes 'Age of demon Kali", where "Kali" of kaliyuga means 'suffering, strife, grieve, hurt' and "Yuga" meaning the last stage of world cycle as per four Yugas described in Sanskrit scriptures. This word basically came from Hindu mythology and describes the time in which spirituality will only be a meaningless word and people will be killing each other for physical and material lust. According to Hindu mythology, this period of kalyug means the age of destruction and will be characterised by degradation of society with rulers levying high taxes, teachings of saints will be fraudulent and far from spirituality, people will be resorting to immoral ways, murders will be reasonless and prayers, worship, devotion, spirituality and God will be just words with no more substance and meaning. When the souls will be empty of morality and the worst of times will reign, then the age of destruction will be at its peak and mark the Kalyug. The mythology marks the beginning of Kalyug during the time of Mahabharata, while the famous astronomer and mathematician, Aryabhatta depicts the commencement of Kalyug in 3102 B.C.E. Today, as the life is becoming advanced, people are losing their credibility, emotions and spirituality. Another meaning of Kalyug is "The age of Machines" which comes from "Kal" meaning "machines" and "Yug" meaning "Era". Kalyug hence also denotes the time where the machines will start to replace humans in work and other spheres of life.

The book Reality of Spirituality in Kalyug brings to surface, the condition of man and society today and concentrates on how people are lead astray in the name of God and spirituality and how the true meaning of both is lost. It also compares today's social spiritual status with that of the past and not only tells us about the difference between the two but also insights about the real truth which is missed by our visionary mind. It reveals the reality of faux spirituality and defines the true meaning of the same. The book questions the blind ideologies and superstition the society is carrying, in their womb of belief. It not only raises doubt on obsolete teachings but also analyses spirituality from a logical and practical perspective.

The book will provoke you to question the wrong practises, negative beliefs and even the real you.

CONTENTS

1. Religious mind wash   1
2. How spiritual gurus fool you   8
3. Our religion is the only religion and rests are not   13
4. Sex is only meant for procreation and not for pleasure   16
5. Homosexuality is a crime and not written in our religious books.   20
6. Woman should be in her boundaries and should obey her man.   24
7. Obey your parents even if they are wrong   27
8. Avoid divorce and tolerate the man even if he is bad as marriage should last till your seven breaths.   30
9. Give whatever you have earned to priests as you will get that back again with interest in your next life   34
10. Donate milk, food, clothes and money to stone idols and see the miracles   38
11. Celibacy   41
12. Keep on chanting the mantras and songs to please god.   47
13. You have to wear this ring or that cloth or that colour for this time to get things right.   52
14. Sex outside marriage is a sin.   56

15.	Liquor and meat is bad for you.	58
16.	Enemies and well wishers are send by God	63
17.	People are getting away from god as they are getting urbanised	66
18.	Material lust	69
19.	A Woman – An Impurity	74
20.	Why people worship god in kalyug?	79
21.	Why people hate god in kalyug?	82
22.	Why people need spiritual gurus, worship houses and religious monuments?	87
23.	The mystery of aliens in kalyug	91
24.	The rebirth theory	100
25.	Does karma work in kalyug?	104
26.	Ghosts and spirits in kalyug.	107
27.	Is God a service provider?	111
28.	Why some are rich and some are poor?	114
29.	Are we following the right procedure to reach God?	117
30.	Who is god?	121
31.	The judgement day	127
32.	The Maya	132
33.	Journey of the soul (Guest Article by Dr. Prerna Singla)	139

Collection
Of Spiritual
Articles That
Will make you
Question the
Religion, the
Being, the
Nature
And
The self.

–Pulkit Mohan Singla, 2016

1
RELIGIOUS MIND WASH...

Religious mind wash is an attempt which can be made by anyone to destroy or weaken any person or group of persons, or even the masses. Generally, such attempts are made by the dictators of different religions and such authoritative religious intellectuals can be found in every religion. The most astonishing thing is that their verdicts are not only obsolete but are ancient in the most orthodox and superstitious manner. The people who follow such dictators are not less in number as fear creates a position of submissiveness. The common people always search for an ideal to make their life perfect like we follow any celebrity or any famous entity who symbolizes success and perfection by their work and life. Similarly, to make our life perfect, most of us follow the people who claim to be the son or disciples of God. We follow them and listen to their ideology and even apply the same in our daily lives to attain peace and perfectness but a wide variety of the dictators are illiterate enough to only feed us with conservative mindset. The most common things which fake gurus or religious dictators educate us are as follows:

- Our religion is the only religion and rests are not.
- Sex is only meant for procreation and not for pleasure.
- Homosexuality is a crime and not written in our religious books.
- Woman should be in her boundaries and should obey her man.
- Obey your parents even if they are wrong.
- Avoid divorce and tolerate the man even if he is bad as marriage should last till your seven breaths.
- Give whatever you have earned to priests as you will get that back again with interest in your next life.
- Donate milk, food, clothes and money to stone idols and see the miracles.
- Practice celibacy to reach God.
- Keep on chanting the mantras and songs to please God.
- Don't ask questions that are raised out of doubt on God's teachings and existence.
- You have to wear this ring or that cloth or that colour for this time to get things right.
- Sex outside marriage is a sin.
- Kill your desires and pleasures and live only for God.
- Avoid western goods and clothing and adopt your nation's assets only.
- Liquor and meat is bad for you.

- Enemies and well wishers are sent by God.
- People are getting away from God as they are getting urbanised.
- Adultery is a sin and prostitutes are sinner.

These are just examples of the nonsense most of the fake gurus or religious dictators teach to mind wash the mango people. Their main concern is the same and that is to create differences through the point of religious supremacy and to create hatred among people of different religions towards each other. These fake gurus are very smart; they incorporate their conservative ideology in the old manuscripts and mythological tales and serve the same to the people like a mix food platter. They remix the old scriptures with their narrow minded notions and create a new song based on biased and discriminatory thinking.

- The questions that these religious mentors fail to answer are as follows:
- Why people worship god in kalyug?
- Why some people hate god in kalyug?
- What is the mystery of aliens in kalyug?
- Does Rebirth exist in kalyug?
- Does karma exist in Kalyug?
- Do ghosts and spirits exist in kalyug?
- Are we following the right procedure to reach God?
- And at the last...
- Who is god in kalyug?

It is observed that these fake gurus also take the help of

some old obsolete laws of British and use the same in their so called religious teachings. Almost every person who attends such religious concerts uses less logic and more superstition as this is what he is being taught since ages via tales chanted by sages and elders. He examines his fellow participant and then another fellow participant and then quickly in a fragment of seconds, he decides that the teaching is coming directly from God and no doubts shall be raised in regards to the same. He remains quiet and listens to the programme very keenly and after regular listing and attendance to such religious concerts, he motivates his ideology towards the ideology of guru. Even if he is a great supporter of women empowerment, he comes home and scolds his daughter, restricting her freedom, inconsiderate about her need to be empowered than to be suppressed, asks her to come home early instead of learning self-defence and advocates her early marriage too. Whatever he has learnt recently dominates his logical and practical ideology and he fights inside his conscious on the topics of religion and reality.

The confusion created by these gurus is so strong that religion seems above every reality and reality seems unnatural to him. Today almost every person is confused and cannot determine what is right and what is wrong. Everyone is hanging on a weak rope whose one end leads to blind religion worship and other end leads to reality and logic. But this does not mean that the common man is stupid. He is smart enough to deal with both the ends and he uses both of them according to the demand and supply rule.

Although, most of the people choose the end point of trusting religion blindly and are destroying their own and others life by old superstitious ideology (Terrorism is a common example); there are still some people who understand that there is God, but even they do not ignore the need of today and the power of realism. They use the term religion for peace but not for changing the lives of others. On the other hand, the fake gurus use religion in opposite manner. Well this constant battle between religion and reality is going on since centuries and there will not be any point of saturation until the fake and fact is clearly understood, distinguished and the latter is applied effectively in Kalyug.

References from scriptures about fake spiritual mentors, showing that even the sacred scriptures do not advocate fake Spiritual Gurus:

The Gunatit Sadhu

'The scriptures say that nishkam, nirlobh, nirman, niswad and nissneh are the attributes of a Sadhu. The Sadhu in whom one observes such attributes has a constant rapport with God. (Gadhada III.27)

'The Sadhu who is venerable enough to be worshipped on par with God lives in a way in which he controls his indriyas and antahkaran, but is not subdued by them. He engages in God-related activities only, strictly observes the Panch Vartamans, realises himself as being Brahman and worships Purushottam. Such a Sadhu can be known neither as a human being nor a demi god, since neither man nor deva possess such attributes. Therefore, such a Sadhu, though he appears to be a human being, deserves to be worshipped on par with God. (Gadhada III.26)

Shreemad Bhagwad Gita

A person is said to be established in self-realization and

is called a yogi [or mystic] when he is fully satisfied by virtue of acquired knowledge and realization. Such a person is situated in transcendence and is self-controlled. He sees everything—whether it be pebbles, stones or gold—as the same. (Chapter 6, Verse 8)

A transcendentalist should always try to concentrate his mind on the Supreme Self; he should live alone in a secluded place and should always carefully control his mind. He should be free from desires and feelings of possessiveness. (Chapter 6, Verse 10)

Holy Bible

Beware of false prophets, which come to you in sheep's clothing, but inwardly they are ravening wolves. Ye shall know them by their fruits. Do men gather grapes of thorns, or figs of thistles? Even so, every good tree bringeth forth good fruit; but a corrupt tree bringeth forth evil fruit. A good tree cannot bring forth evil fruit, neither can a corrupt tree bring forth good fruit. Every tree that bringeth not forth good fruit is hewn down, and cast into the fire. Therefore, by their fruits ye shall know them. Not every one that saith unto me: Lord, Lord, shall enter into the Kingdom of Heaven; but he that doeth the will of my Father which is in Heaven. Many will say to me in that day, Lord, Lord, have we not prophesied in thy name? And in thy name have cast out devils? And in thy name done many wonderful works? And then will I profess unto them, I never knew you: depart from me, ye that work iniquity. (Matthew 7:13–23)

Holy Quran

Allah says: O you who believe! There are indeed many among the priests and the holy men who devour the wealth of others by evil means, and debar the people from the Way of Allah. Give them the good news of a painful torment, who hoard up gold and silver and do not expend these in the Way of Allah. The Day shall surely come when the same gold and silver shall be heated in the fire of Hell, and with it will be branded their foreheads, their bodies and their backs. (And it will be said): Here is that treasure you had hoarded up for yourselves! Taste now the evil of your hoarded treasure! (Chapter 9 Surah Taubah verses 34-35)

2
HOW SPIRITUAL GURUS FOOL YOU?

The easiest way to fool any person is by making him realise that he is the biggest sinner in the whole world. Surprisingly this very job is done by most of the spiritual gurus we have today. They show that they are here to teach us the good things from the book of God but end up making us the ultimate sinner of this world. They don't do this unintentionally, in fact, everything is planned. Today almost every person is facing problems and issues which are either self invited or gifted to us by the people around us, present in the form of friends, enemies, relatives and strangers. We all are dealing with almost exact same issues and same responsibilities. There may be some difference in our background or decision making process but more or less we are the same. The gurus target this sensitive issue of our life and blame us for the same. We are responsible for the issues in our life but every issue cannot be resolved by giving huge donation to the guru or by torturing God with our bitter song of praise or by giving offerings by slaughtering innocent animals (also known as Bali). We end up being a sinner as somehow we couldn't take out time for God, or to understand nature or humanity or the true meaning of good and selfless deed or in many cases we are an atheist. According to these gurus, the atheist is a serious offender and the one who does not acknowledge God is punished for the sins or speaking in their words "An atheist is burnt in hell." The easiest way to fool people is by enumerating the common issues, mistakes and common problems which are linked to human life again and again, for example, "a marriage failed because of incompatibility of stars", "a death happened because of a bad luck", "bad position of stars lead to struggles in work, further leading to failure in accomplishment of great heights". These issues are present in the life of almost every person but when we get to hear what we are suffering, we tend to become more attracted towards the person or the voice we are listening to, without considering facts that death is inevitable and none in the world is born immortal, for every relation to work the couple needs to adapt to the moods and nature mutually, and for every work and everything in life a man must work for it and harder the work sweeter the fruit. The desperation to get easy tips or short cuts to resolve our problems by some supernatural force or divine force magnetically drags us towards the spiritual Gurus just like we eagerly purchase a book related to sex problems when we actually are dealing with some issue related to it. The solutions of these gurus are out of logic and highly superstitious in nature and borders to absurdity for any sane thinking mind (Thinking sanely: an idol of stone, even if absorbs a liquid due to its porosity, has nothing magical in it and if it did, it could have ended the hunger, famine, suffering, starvation in the world with all the things it absorbs). But the argument is further covered with strong counter arguments on superstition creating a never ending vicious web in which people are entrapped (Counter argument: people suffer of starvation, famine because they were sinners in previous births and suffer their karma. One cannot escape the punishment of their bad deeds of previous births but can ameliorate it by donating and doing the so called religious remedies). They create such an ambience of shame and guilt in the minds of people that people are ready to do whatever these gurus suggest, in order to correct their very sins. Such beliefs and mind wash also becomes a potent tool in the hands of people claiming to know black magic and the practiced rituals bring about dangerous manoeuvres which may also include killing of humans to gain personal profits by black magic.

We forget that the ones who are asking us to give up all the material benefits and leisure are also enjoying luxury lifestyle under the cover of ordinary clothes and a pair of spectacles.

They have all the qualities which they ask us to give up, such as anger, envy, hunger, pride, ego and lust. The only difference is that they show these qualities on selective places and we show these qualities ordinarily every time. It is not bad to have a speaker who motivates you towards spiritual awakening but being totally blind in orthodox beliefs is the biggest mistake you will eventually do. People think that giving donations or listening to the guru's misguided teachings will help them delete the sins and mistakes from their life. In simple terms, these gurus advocate that every sin has a material price which we have to pay and we can turn our fate to the best of fates. Surprisingly, they never ask you to pay the donation through a cheque or draft and you never get a receipt out of the amount you paid in their so called donation boxes or centres. The amount so donated by millions of people gets collected and becomes nothing other than the black money. Only God knows where such black money is utilised. Some gurus with such amount start their businesses of manufacturing and selling goods and entrepreneurial giants in the cover of saint.

There is rarely any guru who will advise you to practise humanity besides living and enjoying the leisure and comforts you have earned by your hard work. Instead, they advise you to give up everything whatever you have earned as you will die one day and all those material things won't be carried along. Everybody will die one day, the gurus will as well, but this does not mean that you have to live a life of celibacy and difficulties to reach the God. These all fake things are taught to you by almost every guru. They know that the path they are asking you to follow is really hard and none of us can be free from material comforts and leisure and cannot get rid of the things they render as sins or reasons for sins. As we feel unable to achieve what we are taught, we attempt to rectify the same via some another method and that is to pay for the sins. We feel that by paying, our sins will be waved off or reduced or the guru will do some ritual or some prayer and they will use our money for good and in turn we will get the benefit of the same but it is all useless imagination and blind trust which we are cultivating in ourselves since a very long time.

The fact is that it is impossible to erase our past and the activities we have done in that past. Our future is either a reciprocation of our past or the outcome of our activities. We will pay for what we have done but it will come to us by the course of nature and not by any monetary bribe. If a child won't study for an exam, most likely he will fail. If you drive in the wrong lane, most likely you will have an accident. If you listen to music for long hours chronically, most likely your ear drums will be damaged and may also result in hearing loss. As you do, so shall you receive. It is better to rectify the present by doing good things like practising humanity, tolerance and brotherhood and surprisingly this is what we all can achieve in Kalyug.

3
OUR RELIGION IS THE ONLY RELIGION & RESTS ARE NOT

This statement in itself is a prejudice and partially stated, as it is clearly inconsiderate of different communities and its people and is also advocating religious supremacy in other terms. It is a known fact that God has not made any religion; it's the people who have done this job. We have neither seen nor read any cases or story where different Gods of different religions ever came together to fight for their individual supremacy or worship.

Although different mythological scripts of different communities have portrayed God in different manner but that difference is seen only in the context of name, place and appearance. A notable fact is that every religious book or mythological script advocates humanity, forgives and tolerance. None of them as ever stated that their religion is the only religion or one should not practise this religion or that religion. If such statements have never been recorded in any mythological script or story then, who has bought up this topic? The clear answer is gurus and who is feeding the gurus with all this religious bilge? I guess their mindset and their inner being.

Religion supremacy and religious discrimination goes hand in hand and today almost every saint or guru knows how and when to use this. The policy of divide and rule works magically in this as an outright display of hatred will eventually turn the people violent and preserver for his own religion. They will start to believe that their religion is in danger and will do whatever they can to protect it. This virtual belief is so powerful that humans don't hesitate in killing others in the name of religion. Some sects are busy in increasing their population to increase the volume of people of their religion. Some are exploiting others who do not belong to their religion and some harass others considering their religion superior. In reality, all this is created by faulty teachings by gurus and speeches by leaders who aim for a good political carrier and play the religion card for votes. As they say, the British initiated divide and rule, but the people themselves perfected it. Had there been no underlying division of hearts, it would be impossible to divide all.

It's not required to tell people that we all are born naked, have same colour blood running in our veins and we all will die one day and similar things because everybody is well aware of that. The reality is nobody wants to implement the same in their daily lives. It's not that they don't know things; it's just that they don't consider this a priority.

nother important aspect to muse over is who comes under this ideology. There are millions of people out there who are not advanced in terms of knowledge and education. Besides illiterates, the highly educated ones are also fooled because they have not really soaked the knowledge gained. Most of the time, they have only copied excerpts or paragraphs for exams. Very few among them who have genuinely analysed, learnt and known, can be ascribed as wise knowledgeable people.

Talking about illiterates, they are considered nothing less than an animal who dances on the tunes of people, for food, money and liquor. You can create countless crowds of illiterate listeners by giving some cheap bait, a common strategy most of the politicians apply.

There is no scripture or mythological evidence that shows any record of a religious supremacy over the other. In fact, people have made their own unique image of God to who they worship, meditate, pray and love. Another noteworthy point here is that no matter what name of God, or what religion one worships and follows, the feeling in that worship remains the same. The hope, the pain, the tears, the devotion, and no matter which God or which religion, the devotion in the hearts is unchanged.

Surprisingly, today almost everyone is away from humanity and is doing against the religious scriptures teaching of love, brotherhood and humanity for all. This dual face of human nature if not corrected, will provoke humans to customise God according to their ideology and soon the day will come when humans will lay down their own rules of crime and corruption under the headline "what God has said".

4
SEX IS ONLY MEANT FOR PROCREATION AND NOT FOR PLEASURE

Is it possible to survive without sex? Have you ever considered a life where you make love with your wife for a child and after that you do not touch her again in your entire life or never feel the sexual urge at all? Is it possible to detect that a particular session of making love will make her conceive or not? Is making love a crime even if you are married?

The one who says that sex is only meant for procreation is a foolish and most irrational person in the world. Surprisingly, there are many gurus who say that, and this statement is given to make people realise that they are sinners. By saying so, they generate a sense of fear and guilt in the minds of people and to get rid of such a sin, people devote themselves to trying out spiritual remedies and some even forcefully abstaining themselves from physical love, resulting in depression, sexual frustration and many similar conditions. And if some of us are enjoying extra marital affairs or being single, also fulfilling our sexual need then we are labelled as the most evil person on earth according to some religious gurus.

Again, I don't have to give any logic behind the statement of these gurus because this statement is seriously beyond superstition. The human body is designed to have sex and in absence of the same the body suffers mentally, physically as well as emotionally. Otherwise too, it is a matter of common sense to ponder upon the fact that if God wanted us to abstain from physical pleasures, he would have created such a body need only immediately before conceiving and that should have ended forever right after the child is born. But nothing of sorts happens, in fact, women attain menopause when they start to advance towards her sixties while men are known to have the sexual ability even at a later age.

There are millions of families and couples who turn their life to hell by abstaining from sex in their lives. Every creature of the planet bears the urge to make love with its partner. Just like there is need to breathe, excrete, and eat, there is a need to make love. We do not acquire it. It is gifted to us by nature.

Also, there are no scriptures or evidences that advocate validity of sex for procreation only. Many have said that one should control excessive appetite for sex, which is again an example of the statement "Excess of everything is bad", but an interesting fact to consider is that many mythological tales mention that almost every God who incarnated on earth in human form enjoyed physical love making for pleasure apart from procreation and even that in those times when God was on earth, there was a tradition among the kings to have countless wives and courtesans at their disposal. There are even temples and monuments demonstrating the power and importance of sexual activities, which we consider today as rich history. Then why physical love is still an issue and a taboo for human beings?

Physical love was also practised by almost every king or queen from historical times and there were numerous wars and alliances done between kingdoms for love and love making. Things are same today as well; the only difference is modernization, civilisation and advancement of technology and lifestyle. Today people are more liberal and broad minded because they understand the importance of life and surely the key to happiness. But as the development and developing minds are raising the level of their stepping stones there are many out there ready to encumber your liberty, providing for you a competitive and a submissive environment since if all become kings, then who will be the Kingdom?? Obviously, the kingdom has to be the common man and their need to stay on top, to be worshipped, is met by being kingly as they too desire limelight and so the position of hurdle creator is being filled by gurus and mythical political leaders today who label and advocate sex as unethical while enjoying the very same themselves.

Many religious mentors, in the cloak of worship misguide women and subject them to serve them in the name of service to the almighty. You can say guru worship is nothing but a code word for sexual exploitation. There are many cases of rape, assault , sexual crime that have come into the limelight, in which the devotee has pressed sexual exploitation charges against gurus but things still work at their course. Contradictory to their teachings, besides teaching against sex, they are more prone to sexual crimes, but again, it's very hard to detect the list of their acts as they are protected by the guards of spiritual doors.

The more foolish the statement, the more the limelight they gain. This very phenomenon is shared not only by the gurus but also by the politicians who advocate such gurus. There have been cases where couples in parks or public places are harassed for being intimate and leaders try to squash the liberty of people by banning pornography. Such numerous acts send to the world, a message of hatred towards physical love making and are nothing but attempts to suppress the physical needs of the body inconsiderate of the fact that sexual frustrations arising from sexual suppression can lead to psychological ailments like depression, stress, lead to suicides and even crimes like sexual harassment, groping, rapes, marital rapes, infant rapes, family rapes and gang rapes. In other words, it is nothing but a contribution towards making an unhealthy and a crime prone society.

No matter what so ever happens nobody will say NO to sex since it is guided by nature and the body system every creature is born with. We need to understand that sex is a NATURAL body need just like the need to breathe, sleep, excrete and suppressing it will only ruin the life and hence one should, instead of suppressing, attend to the very need in Kalyug.

5
HOMOSEXUALITY IS A CRIME AND NOT WRITTEN IN OUR RELIGIOUS BOOKS

"Homosexuality is a crime and not written in our religious books."

This is the most common statement made by the gurus in order to bind the liberty of homosexual community. The reason behind doing so maybe anything ranging from hatred, orthodox beliefs, created negative image or simple attribution towards going with the crowd. Since ages the very subject had been neglected and even labelled as crime or unnatural. Some nations have liberalised LGBT today but there are countries that still label it as unnatural, an offense, a crime, a psychological disorder, and many such things. Under the same, the people so labelled frequently face hatred, disgust, bullying, are being beaten, disowned punished and even murdered by their family, friends, and society and at some places from the country also.

Apart from the controversial statements, many other things like love, humanity, brotherhood, mercy and truth are mentioned in many religious and spiritual books but these Gurus fail to preach and implement them in their daily lives. In fact, many spiritual mentors can be frequently seen getting involved with politics and live a life that is contrary to those illustrated in the same religious and spiritual books. Some also defend their luxurious lifestyle with the statements that outside of being a guru, they are common people. I wonder what is "Outside being a guru" or does it imply that that being a guru is just like momentary change of clothes along with role playing??

As per the subject of homosexuality is concerned, the mention of homosexuality exist since ages can be found in many religious books. In some, the mythology states stories where the God himself married a man or interchanged the gender role and even stories where the divine is considered a merger of both Divine God and the Divine Goddess. So, if Mythology is to be followed and worshipped, then the concept of homosexuality stands normal and maybe even divine where the aspects of both the divine man and divine woman are known to form the ultimate Lord himself.

But if for instance, we ignore the mythological part, Homosexuality is found in more than 1500 species of the world. There are creatures all over the planet that are known to show homosexual behaviour and are generally known as Hermaphrodites. There are also plants that bear the capability of production on their own (Ferns for example). The hermaphroditism is in no way considered unnatural or psychological disorder but an exception to what is observed in many sexes and reproductions. Whether to produce offspring or not, if hermaphroditism is a natural occurrence in many other species of the planet, how can then it be abnormal or unnatural in the species Homo sapiens??

Homosexuality is a debatable topic because people are still not well educated about it and spread hatred, unacceptability towards the ones belonging to this community. Such poor literacy about our own species results in bad consequences (honour killing, attacks, dehumanising, barbarism and many other tortures by normal people who are otherwise incapable of killing and label themselves as God fearing, pious creatures.)

Poor literacy about social issues is similar to a person flying an aircraft who is only acquainted with controls of a car. A disaster is bound to happen but only applicable to weaker people with no social status or power. For anyone at powerful position, even if belonging to LGBT community, such spiritual gurus never dare to raise a finger at them. But above all, it must not be forgotten that all beings have the right to live with dignity. Sadly, the very right given by the constitutions of the world is easily forgotten.

Certain Spiritual Mentors or gurus claim to cure homosexuality, rendering it a disease or a bad trend adopted from other cultures. I wonder can they cure God who had started such trends according to the mythological tales. Or can they disown God? You never know. Maybe they can. The fact is that most of the Gurus impose upon people, their orthodox thinking, and condition minds to think and believe the same way. They usually link it up with religion or spiritual awakening and easily lead astray. Such Gurus even if read directly from those spiritual books, lack spiritual awakening since they fail to show regard towards Mother Nature and its creations.

Anyone, to be divine, will first have to learn to be human in Kalyug.

6
WOMAN SHOULD BE IN THE BOUNDARIES AND SHOULD OBEY HER MAN

I have attended many religious seminars where the Gurus usually divert their spiritual teachings to the topic of women and their roles in society. They initiate the topic with an example or famous news about women and start giving their so called judgement on the issue like a judiciary and soon their voice is ready to spit out a venomous ideology towards women. In fact, some even cross their limits in this process like in the sensitive cases of gang rapes, spiritual gurus were seen suggesting that the woman should have cooperated with the monsters and should have allowed them to rape her while begging for her life if they would spare. An alarming fact to notice was that the listeners like herds were quietly listening as if it was a word-to-word verdict of God. It was only after the matter attracted media and verdicts ridiculed, the listeners raised objection.

Spiritual teaching first of all has nothing to do with political issues or political involvement. Even if it does, none should pollute the society in the name of God or religion.

The ideologies that advocate surrender to crime than to fight against crime render the image of woman that of a submissive obedient servant working continuously and serving the opposite sex. In such cases, the portrayal of woman as an object not only pollutes the society but also has worse consequences when such mindset is implemented, and it is frequently implemented since the Mouth that is talking is of a guru who holds a position of spiritual mentor and even as God for many of the followers.

Thanks to urbanisation and people of some great ideologies who banned the horrifying ancient practises that were carried in the name of religion and rituals, like sati system was abolished by Raja Ram Mohan Roy. If we had completely relied on these gurus, the majority of female population would have been burnt under the excuse of sati and rest would have been completely enslaved and restricted under the excuse of Purdah or veil or ghunghat, covered under tons of cloths and subject to spending the entire life in four walls of closed rooms.

Although, even today women face torture, harassment, exploitation, bindings and boundaries with their men controlling their life from conduct in public to the clothes they wear, their ideology and self esteem too; It has been seen that the crippled mentality against female gender is generally carried by so called religious mentors who believe that their religion recommends women to be tamed or maintained in a certain way like a pet or a machine which needs to be carefully used.

These gurus who can be rightly called religious

dictators are more active in adjudication of woman clothing suggesting a set pattern of conduct and clothing. The ones, who follow westernised cultures or clothing that is not suggested by these mentors, are frequently tagged as women of faulty character and rightfully deserving punishments like gang rapes or corrective rapes. Not just crippled ideology, some gurus also guide to their devotees, the magic tricks to control the women in their houses. Such content can also be frequently checked on the internet.

People irrespective of the literary rate blindly start to follow and implement such verdicts about life and living of women in society as an attempt to bring back their long lost culture and heritage. It has also been noticed that people who consider women less than man are more active in crimes like domestic violence

If you completely rely on these gurus and their cynical morals you will end up in an environment where there will be no dignity towards women as the concept of male dominant society still governs their crippled minds. With the rapidly changing world, women have discovered their strength and individuality and shall continue to do so and bring further changes in the society.

7
OBEY YOUR PARENTS EVEN IF THEY ARE WRONG

Parents are the creators but does that give them every right to twist and modify your life according to their will? Is obeying parents blindly the right thing to do? Will you go to heaven if you listen to them even if they are wrong?

Worshiping parents like God is written in many scriptures and religious books and there are also many cases in history and mythological tales where some wrong decisions taken by parents turned the cycle of their children in an anti clock wise direction.

Right from birth till their life, our parents nurture us like a gardener nurtures the plant. They feed us, raise us, take care of us, love us and support us in every phase of our life and so we also love our parents like no other. Their love and affection is precious and even the most expensive things stand valueless as compared to their love and affection for us, but are parents also considering our love precious today? Do they also selflessly love the children as they are; no matter what they do or what they like?

It has been seen that almost every child is under the control of his guardian till he starts earning and is married. The time before the self dependence and marriage of the child is generally considered the golden era for parents, since almost every child listens to what his parents tell him and also obeys his guardians with honesty. As soon as the child becomes an independent individual and that too earning, he is able to take decisions about himself, obey his will and pursue his likings. He listens to his beliefs and does what suits him and fosters his thoughts and desires. Choosing partner for marriage is one such thing independent folks do, which sometimes become an issue for the parents. They not only want to decide whom he marries but also want to decide what he purchases and even how he lives his married life.

Parents are not completely wrong as every parent desires for a good fortune for their child so fostering their expectations and needs is important but sometimes the concept of obeying parents go far beyond the reality, which unintentionally leads to serious crimes and awful incidents.

Every parent is not bad but there are many with criminal beliefs and detrimental attitude. They apply this on the lives of their children to accomplish their lost desires. They manipulate and even emotionally black mail their own blood in order to reach their point of so called salvation. This can be seen in many cases where parents and children fight on the issue of marriage. They generally do not accept what their child wants and hence black mail him either emotionally or even threaten him by their disowning strategy. In this way, they ask for the price of love, which is squashing the self serving attitude of the child. They claim the value of their love and affection using emotionally targeting pick up lines like: we have done so many sacrifices for you and we have not brought you up for this day. What they trying to say by this? Are they asking for the pay back of the favours they did in the past? Is the creator asking for the price of his labour?

It has been seen in cases where parents black mail the child, the child may surrender but he loses the emotional bonding and attachment soon. He realises that money and self centeredness is everything as this is what his parents taught him through the meanest lesson ever. The child who is under the control of guardian or dependent on his parents may find the situation worse. In the cases of homosexual or transgender children things may also be beyond detestability.

There are many parents who surrender in front of the gurus and spiritual dictators to get the remedy or tricks to control their child or get him to obey them and the teachings they receive are very destructive which not only ruins the child's present and future, but also tears up the golden memories of the past.

8

AVOID DIVORCE AND TOLERATE THE MAN EVEN IF HE IS BAD. MARRIAGE SHOULD LAST TILL YOUR LAST BREATH

Marriage is the most important event in our life. It not only changes our present but our future as well. All beings desire for an everlasting bond, be it animals or Human beings, irrespective of sexual orientation. However, variations in the bonding patterns are seen in both animals and humans.

You must be wondering what the connection of marriage with spirituality is. We believe that the marriages are made in heaven and so most of the cultures leave no stone unturned into making sure that the marriage alliance is made in heaven. For the same, we generally do everything that can assure that the marriage is a heavenly alliance. Included in these are horoscope match making, predictions via oracles and tarot cards, background check via hired detectives, medical check-up for anomalies and status of fertility and/or virginity, examination of financial capacity and even long-term dating. The bride's family usually adopt horoscope matching and background checks while the groom's family usually adopt background check ups and medical check-ups. After the things are set from both sides, the alliance is turned into marriage.

It is assumed that marriage is the licence to happiness and a boy becomes a man after a marriage. Some of the most important things that must be considered while match making are blindly ignored, like behaviour, compatibility, chemistry, morals, ideology and even the taste. It is difficult to notice these elements in arranged marriages and in the very first meeting since at such events; it is easy to portray the character of an ideal match. Secondly, less conversation or less time given to the couples before marriage also creates a situation of confusion and fake assurance. We generally rely on the horoscope which is generally linked to the spiritual platform. The ones who advocate long- term dating as a justified step towards marriage alliances are generally considered a fool as people consider traditions above intuition. We get so excited to get married that the demerits are covered under the pomp and show and ostentatious display of glitters and lights.

While the families are lost in the baseless discussions on wedding dresses or overfluous arrangements, the most important issue of knowing the counterpart is further neglected in the process. Most of the families are so orthodox that they don't send their daughters for a date with the groom prior to marriage. They believe that less is more and hence the lesser the divulging of true self, the more the chances to make marriages work. The mistake of blurting out anything irrelevant or about past romances may become the reason for rejection. Hence, it is advocated that minimum information must be revealed and by all means every attempt should be made to answer only in a 'Yes' or 'No', if at all necessary. Most of the time marriages fail due to either miscommunication or less communication and the excessive dependency on gurus and priests for the remedies to a happy married life, serve to worsen the situation. In the age of technology, living with orthodox notions lead to issues and gaps only.

It has been seen that, in the absence of good acquaintance with the future husband, women have been trapped in the most disastrous marriages where she gets a monster in the shape of a husband. He beats her, rapes her and even feeds on her income and this torture continues till her last breath. Some husbands with a suspicious mindset frequently raise questions on the character of their wives, especially on the ones who are employed. Apart from this, there are cases where a man gets a woman of hot temperament, incompatible with his very nature and excessively suspicious of his activities. Things become worse when a gay man or an impotent man is gifted to the bride with the price tag of sorrows and fights. Such cases are countless and generally end in lifelong sorrows and pains.

It is a shame that parents advocate their children to tolerate and live in such marriages and those women are generally the main sufferer who are asked to cooperate no matter how much her husband beats her. The honoured parents feel shame in keeping their divorced daughters since a label of divorce is not considered good in society and the image of the girl deteriorates and therefore, she is thrown away at the disposal of the demons where she has to suffer and also retain the tag of 'married happily ever after' for all her life.

Although, now-a-days with modernisation, things have changed a lot, but not yet completely improved.

Generally, such ideology of painful adjustments in every possible circumstance comes from superstitious mindset laid down by gurus and from people who are still living the life of orthodox beliefs. A situation is created where woman freeing herself from sick marriage is labelled as that of bad character due to which she was left by her husband. Such circumstances become a matter of shame even for the parents and they deny sheltering their own girl and if the girl is dependent one, then she has no way out than to keep suffering all her life. Some people also believe that second marriage will again be a matter of useless investment.

Although today the practical generation is avoiding such superstition and are quitting the ugly relationships but still the power of superstition still haunts the life of many couples and is worsened by the spiritual mentors who exploit people in the name of religion and spirituality. I firmly believe that the solution to this is to educate our daughters and sister and help them be self-dependent and teach them to tolerate no evil. If unfortunately, the girl is trapped with such a husband, then parents should support her and she, with her education should be able to live independently with dignity.

9
GIVE TO THE PRIESTS WHATEVER YOU HAVE EARNED AND YOU WILL GET MULTIFOLDS IN YOUR NEXT LIFE

I have heard this line many a times and it is often said when a priest or guru is conducting a seminar and there is huge crowd jumping and squashing each other feet's to have their one look. The golden box of treasure is generally placed in front of the stage where everybody donates some amount. The announcement is generally bold when the priest and his messengers announce emphasising to donate all their savings to the priests for God, and assure that they will get back multifolds of the donated amount in their next life with the bonus award that their sins will be erased or decreased.

The People blindfolded in the name of God and religion and mostly selfishly in an urge to wipe away their sins donate large amounts of their hard earned money. Apart from that they are persuaded to purchase worship items and religious books from the counters opened at the seminar premises by these gurus. Not just that the day's earning is proudly announced as the mount donated for God, praising the devotion of people towards their religion & God, often with the dialogues like "oh my children! Today's donation for God has crossed the billion. The God is very happy to see positive and philanthropic changes in you."

Although Politicians play a major role in the success of these gurus as these gurus get large acres of land at very cheap rates in the name of religion or for establishing worship houses, but the role of public cannot be neglected too. The people are the main source through which they earn money and that too in billions. People generally believe in following the one who is successful and when a guru becomes famous people follow him blindly because they believe that he is more genuine and his remedies more effective, that is why a huge crowd follows him and so he is a true magical or divine guru who will help them to get rid of sins. They believe that this monetary investment or donation will work as a perfect price to erase their sins or wave off bad consequences of their bad deeds. After all, what can't be bought in this world? Everything. Then why not buy good luck and fate?

But this investment is useless as there is no specific definition to sin because according to all religious books killing , hurting, cheating, lie, adultery, meeting with a man/woman other than yours, bribe, dowry, and even earning more profit is a sin. Some religious books even illustrate the kind of horrible punishments a person will be subjected to, in hell. While some other illustrate how prophets of God paid the price of people's sins. But one fact inevitably exists is that almost everything is counted under sin. You kill a fish; you are a sinner because killing is a fish. You cut a tree; you are a sinner because killing/hurting is sin. But then I wonder, when we walk on the ground we kill millions of creatures which are otherwise invisible to our naked eyes, and even the visible ones like ants, cockroaches, spiders are killed. Can you ever be free of sin?

There are now-a-days huge taxes levied on common man that from eating to clothing to living, his life is hugely taxed and there are many people on the planet who, in this Kalyug era of corruption and scams, tries to save his few hundred bucks by stealing from the government i.e. by not paying all his taxes. I leave the decision upon the readers as to which is higher stealing: scams worth billions and trillions or a few stolen hundreds?? But in both scenarios, can people ever be free of sin??

One can never be rid of sin according to the various things the religious books consider as sin, so the possibility of a hundred percent goodie life is impossible. The only people who enjoy good days with the enormous collected money are such religious and spiritual mentors who con people in the name of sin, by inducing fears in people. It wouldn't be wrong to say that priesthood or profession of guru is indeed the most prosperous and highly profitable business today with no chances of recession and the most saddening truth is that the donators in such seminars are basically poor or middle class community who are already struggling with their lives.

The business of Priesthood succumbs to a few basic things which are crucial moral requirements of any being, like, love, friendship, love of living and fear of death, desire to get rich or successful, desire of good career and big money or fame, fear of losing someone or something, and many similar things which are common to every person. The atmosphere and ambience is created so deep and related that people are compelled to trust the words of these gurus and speakers and are thus easily lead astray. Apart from donation, some gurus also charge fees for the solution of each person's problem or to give them personal codes of reaching God.

An amazing thing to hear is that almost every person who pays for the solution of their problem admits to be satisfied and relived from the problem they have been facing. Some invest hugely in Horoscopes, some in Tarots, Crystal Balls, some in Numerology, some believing in the magical powers of the Guru to talk to God, some even opt for Black Magic to resolve their problems. Most of these predictions are either based on set patterns, or are generated via computerised software or have a balancing set of statements (Like, You have money on your cards today, but you will get it only by hard work. Obviously, if you work hard for something, you gain.)

And such business of spirituality or getting you salvation is mostly a con trick, and the business flourishes on the supernatural beliefs of people. Without much investment for advertising and promotions, people themselves serve to Promoting such Gurus, The 'Word of Mouth' publicity being the most effective and authentic tool. The Owners of such businesses gain the status of Divine and are blindly worshipped for almost all life and even after that. The manufacturing units started in the name of religion and spirituality soon hit billions of turnovers in the market, but becomes tax exempted because everyone has the right to preach religion. So if you are looking for good business start-up, simply priestly clothing may do the trick for you too. But certainly won't get you God or salvation in Kalyug.

10
DONATE MILK, FOOD, CLOTHES AND MONEY TO STONE IDOLS AND SEE THE MIRACLES

Donating milk, clothes, money and food is a very common practise carried out since years and different places have different beliefs in this. Some practises can be considered extreme where devotees donate hairs, blood, liquor and even practise animal sacrifice for the fulfilment of one's wish. The tradition is so powerful that almost every person believes and practises this but the irony is that the one who receives such gifts of hair, liquor, blood, is either a stone idol or a monument or a slab.

With the donation of food items and clothes, although, people believe that after an initial ceremony of worship the same is distributed to poor or given to priests but the ground reality is very different from the assumption. The very issue is covered in many movies and documentaries worldwide and shows that tons of milk is wasted every year in the name of ritual and so the food, while, in case of animal sacrifice millions of animals face brutal death in the name of worship and celebration. Such acts may appear sad as well as entertaining or humorous to others but those who perform this are very sensitive and serious about it.

The ritual of gifting food, cloths, liquor, blood and life of an innocent creature, is also commenced by the so called priests and gurus to earn a good scale of income and choice of items through superstition. The corruption reaches its peak when they demand bed, clothes, mobile and even ornaments in the name of the dead whose crimination ceremony they conduct. A common excuse these priests generally make for obtaining such materialistic things is that our loved one will get these things, for use, in the afterlife or in their new life and people believe this fact intensely.

It has also been observed that tons of gold ornaments and other expensive metals are donated to adorn stone idols. None of these assets are donated to poor for the betterment of their life or in the least to help them in some way, and enormous money so donated is accumulated in these worship houses. A remarkable thing to note is that the stone idols are embellished with golds while the living human is left to die on streets; innocent creatures are slaughtered brutally in the name of beliefs. Is it not the food for thought that worships like this is not worship in true sense but only a means to accumulate enormous wealth by befooling people and playing with their emotions? If such enormous money is utilised for the wellbeing of the society, the Government will have no need to take loans from overseas or foreign banks. Such things clearly prove that the Nation is not poor, but the intentions of doing good are faux, such definitions of worship and such created rituals that are used to only accumulate money and materialistic things are not worship or devotion but fraudulence.

It is sad to know that non-living things are offered so many things in kalyug besides the fact that millions are still sleeping empty stomach, millions are dying of starvation and of extreme weather conditions, millions are begging outside such worship houses, eating from dustbins and sleeping under the empty sky with almost none of the basic amenities, left to die while the worship houses shine emotionlessly with the brightest of lights.

11
CELIBACY

Is it really possible for a human to celibate entire life for their religion or belief in the God? It may sound strange today but as we have read in many ancient mythological tales and scripts there were people, who believed in this phenomenon, advocated as well as practised celibacy in their life. According to the Oxford Dictionary, Celibacy is the state of abstaining from marriage and sexual relations: a priest who had taken a vow of celibacy.

It is often in association with the role of a religious official or devotee, but considering the current scenario where every other Spiritual mentor is being charged with exploitation of his devotees, things are changing and it is almost impossible to see anyone following celibacy in the truest manner. Most of us link celibacy with being unmarried but there are unmarried people who enjoy the pleasures of married life and family, without being in the commitment with one partner. A general mentality being carried now-a-days is that being married to one partner is like being bounded and the freedom encumbered. On the other hand, Live in relationships give the freedom to walk out of that relationship by will or easily if the alliance doesn't work out and also opens opportunities to link up in another affair without much legal implications or tantrums of family or liability of children (except if one himself wishes to settle down in a matrimonial alliance). The trend is so on today that youngsters frequently adopt the "casual affairs" or "live-in" as an alternative or the label under which they portray to their families of being a celibate until the marriage is fixed with someone. Only some couples walk past the state of casual affairs and enter into marriage with the same person who they label as their girlfriend or boyfriends.

The Gurus today advocate celibacy and they also give us the references of the same from the mythological scripts as proofs and evidences but are they really logical? They say that sex is a bad thing to do and it makes you dirty. Not only that, some families also abstain women from worshipping God when they are in their menstrual cycles or after they have made love with their partner, not even allowing them to come anywhere near the worshiping place. It is also a famous belief that when a person enters a married life, he becomes selfish since the responsibilities to full fill family needs and to accomplish the family roles he adopts unfair means and does not even hesitate to commit crime and corruption but this statement is contrary to the fact that one does not need to be married to commit crime, and in fact, the status of married or single has nothing to do with a person's tendency to commit crime. This is also true with age, gender, ethnicity, or any other criteria on which such things are claimed. An age of immaturity or as we say "Juvenile" age does not guarantee that a person will be pure as divine. Crime is present everywhere on the planet irrespective of the religion, caste, creed, race, sex, gender or orientation of a being. Having said that, the preference to celibacy to attain God and the claim that celibacy keeps the mind, body and soul clean seems to lose its credibility. On top of that, the increase in sexual frustration, depression, and sexual crimes arising as direct outcomes of the same, cannot be ignored.

It is impossible to reach God through celibacy. Many spiritual practices including Meditations, spiritual awakenings, Kundalini, Extra-sensory perceptions etc., includes the sexual channel as the first channel for the spiritual energy to pass through a being and that one cannot attain complete spiritual awakening without opening the sexual channels. Likewise, we have never seen God appearing and advocating against making love and asking us to abstain from the very same throughout our lives to reach him or stay single as a proof of purity. Scientifically speaking, each body, be it animals or plants bear a system that guides the working of the human machine and makes sure that the basic requirements of air, water, food are met, for the body to survive and sustain. THE BODY GUIDES THE BEING; THE BEING DOES NOT GUIDE THE BODY. Similarly, there is a system and cycle of reproduction guided by hormones. Right from the fragrance of the body to visual signals to sexual attractiveness of a being to falling in love to making physical love to reaching orgasm to release of dopamine in the body, all is channelled in a pre-defined, unchanging, repetitive cycle that facilitates sexual meeting of two beings. In most of the species, the way of love making is same, i.e. unison of the male and the female counterparts. The only thing that changes is the manner in which reproduction or procreation occurs in different species, with some beings reproducing asexually by splitting, budding or fragmentation while others sexually by giving birth to their progeny or laying eggs.

Homo sapiens are among the very species that reproduce by giving birth. But, worth a thought here is the fact that if human was created only for procreation and not for sexual pleasure, then the Human body would have been created and designed to give birth to their progeny only by asexual reproduction and not by sexual reproduction. Thinking about the second aspect of this fact, according to the beliefs on being a celibate to attain God, the organisms that are reproducing asexually are closest to attaining God since they are only procreating to give birth to their progeny and also abstaining from sex at the same time.

It will be a foolishness to question the role of an organ in a body, since it is another well known fact that the organs or body parts that are useless or used less, are eliminated over years in the process of evolution or are reduced to being the vestigial or rudimentary organs (Like the tailbone in humans, vermiform appendix in humans, male mammae, wings of some flightless birds, hind legs or pelvic rudiments in some reptiles like snakes, stipules and carpels in plants). It clearly refers to the fact that the body is vigilant enough to eliminate the parts that it renders useless to its needs. If making physical love was useless to the body need, it would have been long eliminated or reduced to being a rudimentary organ.

It is a well established fact that the human female bears about one to two million immature follicles that are turned into ova and later to eggs. While, a human male is known to ejaculate 180-400 million sperms per ejaculation and has the power of libido for almost whole life span. In a human female, if suppose, menarche commences at the age of 13 yrs and menopause at the age of 55; she has about 42 years of active sexual age. In that active sexual age, pregnancy over 35 years of age is not recommended by doctors due to another well known fact that reproduction after 35 years of age has high chances of pregnancy complications, ectopic pregnancy, still births, chromosomal or other defects in the babies that are born. So, roughly speaking, the total number of years in which a woman can give birth to a child accounts to 20 yrs (13-35), while the total number of years she is sexually active is 42 (13-55), yet the world average fertility rate is 2.5 births per woman (World bank stats between 1960 to 2012). If the human body is designed only for procreation then either the menopause should have commenced right after giving birth to a couple of babies or the body would have been designed to bear only some hundred follicles, enough to birth to a couple of babies. Clearly, the human body is designed for much more than just procreation.

Similarly, with human male body, if there was no need for sexual intercourse as a means for pleasure, then the body would have no active sexual systems working for almost all life and the human body, in absence of sexual pleasures, would not sink into sexual frustration or depressions owing to which a human easily commits the crimes like rapes, exploitation and other unfair means to fulfil these body needs or sometimes even commits suicide.

Again, it will be a foolishness to say that the body is created only for physical love or only for procreation when the body is designed to serve multiple purposes and one must be able to fulfil these basic body needs. So next time a guru asks you to abstain from making love, you know how to reply to his illogical statements in Kalyug.

12
KEEP CHANTING THE MANTRAS AND THE SONGS TO PLEASE THE GOD

We all worship God in a certain way either by chanting mantras or by singing the songs of praise and our needs and wishes are also same. Most of us only chant mantra or sing the songs of praise to get our work done. So it clearly looks like a bribe rather than a true devotion. It becomes impossible for us to keep worshipping God everyday without asking for anything in return. Even in our holy prayers we are asking something or the other from the Almighty.

The fulfilments of our wishes have a direct impact on our devotion. When our wishes are fulfilled or we get the things that we covet, we automatically connect it with the miracles of God and say that God has responded to our prayers. The rituals or manoeuvres we do become the tried and tested tricks to get our works done by God. Only investment that is required are few things that we offer to God and the songs we sing. In some worship rituals, a ritual is not rendered complete without offering some money to God too either in the name of God or in the name of Philanthropy..

Regularly doing the same, we become so habitual of

expecting the unexpected or attaining the results miraculously without even working towards the same since our firm belief stands that God can do any miracle.

I still remember the same things when applied by parents and also by kids before exams and results. "Pray to God. He can only pass you. Even if you don't study and leave the sheet blank, if God is happy with you, a wild wind will blow the answer sheets and they will pass you on passing credit. Or in the least, God will turn the professor's mind while he checks your answer sheet. So pray, praise and please God before exams and results." These are the words of one of my uncles who guided me this when I was very small. Only today I know that one must prepare well to excel.

I had also chanted mantras during my school days after I passed in exams one after the other. Every time I passed my belief in the fact strengthened that the worship mantras work. The pile of my belief grew so large and got so strengthened, that studying for exam seemed non-sensical to me. One can always keep chanting the mantra and will pass like always, and I did once. I did not prepare the subject I had disliking for and spent almost all day chanting Mantra. You all can guess the result. I failed. And that was when I realised that one MUST also work hard. Belief in God is not wrong, but treading deals for personal benefits, Singing songs and offering materials with no hard work will certainly not get you things. It is high time, the essence of worship is to be realised. People do not know what devotion is, what worship is, and today they are doing these blindly under the label of piousness.

The same happened to my sister when my mother passed away. Right before her death, my sister chanted all mantra possible, did all ritual possible. But mother died and my sister exclaimed, "God betrayed me. He betrayed my trust, and my devotion." Apparently at that age of thirteen years our mind was too young to explore and understand the meaning of God, worship and devotion beyond what was taught to us at home. Today as a doctor she knows that when a human body system is failing, the body is bound to die. As a lover of philosophy she knows that what begins is destined to end. But the process took lot of learning, lot of awakening to the worldly truths and lot of effort for walking towards truth. It could have been avoided, if we were taught the true meaning right from childhood than the fiction like world of Magics of God stories.

In kalyug, most of the priests succumb to this weakness of being and plays the "Tales of Magical God" trick to fool their devotees, and since those are so closely knit to the happenings in real life, we instantly connect the happening to a miracle and become the loyal and blind devotee.

Most of the religious and spiritual speeches contain instances and stories that explain that one must praise God to get things done. They also teach us that the non-believers or atheists are punished or sent to hell. And many others claim how a devotee or worshipper got their works done, met a love of life, got their business or work successful and even attained salvation. Such misguidance also become basis of criminal activities where people resort to criminal activities and criminal mind set only to achieve salvation and place in heaven, after they die.

He needs to understand that prayer is made for inner peace, meditation, spiritual awakening and not for the enrichment of endless lust and desires.

Some saints even state that the God asks only to worship and to leave everything onto him and that he will also take their sins on himself. Doesn't that serve to create a belief that even if the people kill someone and leave it onto God, they will be free of the sin??? And so if we move towards a higher perspective of the same argument, are terrorists not doing almost the same thing? Killing people in the name of religion and yet they claim that they will be provided salvation and a place in heaven. Their dictators teach them that the lives they are taking are for the protection of their religion and as they are doing all this for their God, they are free from all the sins. They kill and they are confident that their God will forgive their sin for being devoted to him and so they will enjoy a place in heaven. These people are so sightless spiritually that they don't think before they leap. What if every person in the world is fed with a firm belief of such verdicts?? It will serve to create the worst of mankind.

This is another aspect to such verdicts that can easily be understood via televisions, plays, dramas and movies. The story mostly involves a hero, his beloved, love, a bad man and war. Such stories mostly end with the climax where the hero kills the bad man or villain who represents evil, demon, bad thing or person. The hero represents good things and good person just like in epic stories where the Character of God is like character of hero in movies. The message such plays and movies deliver is victory of good over bad, truth over lie, God/hero over demon/villain, where the villain is killed in the end. People are fond of happy endings and second the good God side mostly, but there is another thing they learn: "It is OK to kill a demon/villain or bad man."

They don't learn that they can be all humble, Godly people, but instead learn that the only way to punish the bad one is by killing him. There are countless criminal cases where people have taken law in their hands in the name of heroism. If you investigate/interview them, most of them will be found inspired by the movies and by the stories of the God. They will feel no guilt, no remorse, no shame or embarrassment for taking a life since most of them firmly believe that killing a demon is not wrong but well justified. Now a days, many people have started to commit such crimes in the name of aggressive avatar of Gods and Goddesses. Like their God did in the religious stories, they did for peace harmony, truth, justice. The theory seems nice and justified but is ridden with two major drawbacks:

1. The judicial system of the country will lose its value if such things continued.

2. Each person defines "Bad" in his own way. For some smoking is offensive, for some usage of coprolalia, for some staring is bad and for some even a loud voice or overtaking is bad. If for every bad, people started to kill; the society will be in a huge mess and humanity will lose its existence forever.

That is why today in Kalyug it is very important to understand concepts and apply them wisely for the benefit of mankind and not for mass destruction. Prayers do give us peace, mental calmness and satisfaction but expecting out of the logic miracles by this is seriously an act of Satyug which we are falsely performing in Kalyug.

13
YOU HAVE TO WEAR THIS RING OR THAT CLOTH OR THAT COLOUR FOR THIS TIME TO GET THINGS RIGHT

These are the most common remedies we hear almost every day by gurus either on television or in newspapers or even in real world. All of us have tried these things at least once in our lifetime. Wearing favourite colour or lucky pearl are common remedies, tried in an attempt to make our lives happy, successful and to gain profits along with wiping out the negativity. These attempts are considered optimum because they are really easy to perform, are economical and risk free. Most interesting of them all is zodiac which is often read in the newspaper columns featuring daily or weekly horoscopes along with handy remedies for making the best of our day. But do they work? And do they really have a spiritual connection?

Most of the horoscopes and zodiac theories are based on calculations and set predictions. Even a slight difference or error in the calculation can transform and present a totally different picture of your predicted fate.

Most of the people believe that these things work and the reason behind this is inside our mind. The moment we are told that a ring or a remedy will bring good fortune to us, we instantly perform the trick or wear the ring with a firm positive belief that it will help us succeed in various fields of our life. This magical concept of shortcuts elaborated by the gurus makes us psychologically hyper active and sensitive to the events in our life. It is embedded in our minds so deeply that we do not consider it dangerous in any way.

Sometimes these predictions and horoscopes create an addiction and people spend their entire day in these. They even check the horoscope before stepping outside the house, commencing a work, during a work and this addiction makes them dependent on these predictions in such a way that they no longer enjoy life to the fullest. The entire world seems dangerous to them and for every problem they seek the solution through these remedies. If something wrong happens with them, they quickly change the existing guru and hire another guru for better results. They also create a phobia for some colours because the guru has asked them to avoid a certain colour that is destined to bring them misfortune. They invest good amount of money on rings and jewellery that are known to protect them from evil eye. All these attempts are for those who don't want to work hard in life and depend on shortcuts, magic tricks and remedies.

These tricks may provide a psychological relief but they cannot transform life or get the works done for you. There exist people who are a living proof of the fact that the world has developed and advanced by hard work and not by these magic tricks. Shortcuts only make you dumb and weak. Have you ever read about any legend that became a legend only by doing these tricks all his/her life, wasting time in attempts to shine in the sky? In reality, they worked very hard and lived with good and bad times. They did whatever best they could for survival.

Excessive dependence on these remedies or tricks weakens the mind by creating excessive phobia for even the simplest things, which in turn affects your strength and ability negatively. Apart from wasting time in the devotion to these remedies, we also end up doing things that seem to make no sense. The tricks mind washes your intelligence and level of creativity and force you to consider everything from an angle of superstition and miracles.

Like the tobacco addict gains a brief pleasure in every puff of the cigarette he smokes, an addict to these remedies experience a similar sense of hope and positivity that dies out soon. And to keep gaining those profits the devotee is entangled in a never ending vicious web of magical remedies.

Once you start banning these kinds of fake beliefs and orthodox treatments, you will start to feel very light and fearless. No trick is as effective as an honest dedication to your work. Everything requires hard work and it is obvious to meet difficulties in life and career. The reason behind the complexities in our life is the people. Every person has a different mindset and ideology which they will not change for you. It will be your choice to either adjust yourself or rebel and in this era of urbanisation and technology you must as well keep your principles technologically advanced. Plan ahead, make a proper to-do list, keep alternatives and be well connected. Besides that you need to invest some of your time for others. You may also need their time in future. This world does not work with wonders and miracles. You will get what you offer to the world. There is no free lunch, dinner or breakfast. There exists no life without problems, issues of survival and fear. We all are travelling in the same ship. The difference only exists in our mindset and our actions. Some make right moves and succeed while; some make wrong choices and are defeated.

Many would argue that it's easy to give 'be good" lectures to others than attempting the same but I say it is always better to give it a try at least once before declaring permanent defeat. When the conditions are adverse and there seems no scope for hope, our sensitive heart starts to believe that the shortcuts or remedies or rings or magic tricks or predictions hold the key to our success but in reality these are more non-preternatural then we assume. It's better to think positive and never lose hope or surrender yourself to the misleading, mind boggling, mystic concepts in the age of kalyug.

14
SEX OUTSIDE MARRIAGE IS A SIN

Sex is the most beautiful body need that is coveted but every creature of this world. Apart from being desired by humans and animals, sex is known to be desired by many Gods and Goddesses. Some cultures even have Gods of love, beauty, sexual pleasures, Gods of fertility and even angels who grant the ultimate blessing for a pleasurable life.

In many cultures, sex is worshiped and so the genitals, being the main reason of human evolution then why sex has such a bad social repute. Many gurus regard sex to be a bad thing and if it is done outside marriage it is considered an awful sin. Although, sex outside marriage reflects badly in the society, stands for betrayal in relationships, uncontrollable lust and heights of self centeredness but sometimes this self serving attitude looks justified. There are countless marriages where sex is absent either due to an impotent husband or an ignorant wife or even because the love is no longer alive in relationships. Sometimes it is even due to distinctive ego and ideologies. Such marriages with no sexual pleasure on the cards become a nightmare where living without love becomes less like a life and more like a duty prison. The marriages then survive only by extra marital affair as the wife who is trapped with a gay husband may save her marriage as well as foster her need by dating men outside marriage.

Some cultures advocate coping up with the marriage and living with what they have got. Such plentiful marriages have the couples quarrelling and living like enemies where apart from responsibilities they carry unfulfilled desires of mind, body and soul. The gurus, who advocate that sex outside marriage as sin, do not have any solution for the complicated marriages where things do not work out easy. But in cases where the lust exceeds morality and integrity, besides having a good married life if the partner avails extra-marital pleasures, the same is considered unfaithfulness, cheating, betrayal and immoral. Where the couples lead a good married life and heartily indulge in sexual pleasures but are unable to achieve satisfaction from their partner; they must communicate the issue with them instead of betrayal under the excuse of over powering needs.

Many people indulged in extra-marital affairs are unhappy with their marriages and even after confrontations, regular doctor visits, discussions and total rejections, when all the attempts fail; they by themselves open the doors to extra-marital affairs.

We cannot label it a sin in all cases. Even Gods are known to have many wives. The kings of ancient times too had sex outside marriage with pride and via well defined system which was fostered through courtesans. Sex is not bad but we must remember that it also sets some moral and legal boundaries for us in Kalyug.

15
LIQUOR AND MEAT IS BAD FOR YOU

Liquor and meat are the two forms of food that are always debatable. Some cultures advocate abstaining liquor and meat but some allow it as a part of life. It all depends on ones liking. As we have good majority of vegans and vegetarians, we also have large meat consuming population too. Talking about liquor, it is consumed by both vegetarians and non-vegetarians. But the consumption of meat is prohibited by many religions since animal slaughtering is considered immoral, brutal and a sinuous act. Some religions also support animal sacrifice for worshipping and also enjoy the feast at the time of festivals.

But there is a twist to the above philosophy. Not just any animal is slaughtered. Animals also face discrimination on the basis of species and sex. In some cultures where specific animals achieve deific status and are hence prohibited from slaughtering, in some other cultures the same animal may be a favourite choice, slaughtered in huge number for their meat and leather. There is no prohibition on the eating of all animals (irrespective of species) around the world.

This selective slaughtering is also linked to superstitious beliefs and the Gurus frequently target animals in the name of religion, advocating slaughtering of some and protection of some. This biased advocacy reflects upon lack of knowledge and ignorance of the fact that all creatures are alike and are innocent lives not meant for brutal slaughter. While in some cultures, animals like snakes, tigers, dragons, elephants and cows are worshipped, in others the same may be of no importance and regarded ordinary animals suitable to be killed for meat or leather. I haven't come across anyone fighting for the rights of fishes or chickens, who are mercilessly eaten by millions. Is it because they are not deified by any culture?? We have 8.7 million estimated species in the world (A 2011 study by PLoS Biology estimates 8.7million +/- 1.3 million eukaryotic species on Earth) and we are still counting and no one has managed to weigh the right role of these creatures.

Another set of thinkers might argue against the religious philosophies too. Animal consumption may be considered a sin in some human cultures, but in the Animal kingdom, the same is a part of food chain. A tiger must kill a lamb for the survival of his family and the lamb must run for his own life. The struggle becomes the right to survival each creature is born with. In the same way, if a man is lost in a forest and his survival is at stake, he resorts to killing animals for his survival. Many sects argue that human species being hierarchised as an animal, meat eating for them is nothing but another means to procure food, just like any other omnivorous species. Our semblance to the species of monkeys also point at our semblance in eating habits. Hence, it would be unnatural to restrict one species of the animal kingdom from its normal natural behaviour.

The religious verdicts state that animal slaughter for food is a sin. If all creatures on the planet are divided into two categories, viz. Plants and animals, then shouldn't human slaughter by animals be considered sin too??? And if it is justified for one species, should it not be justified for the other species too?? If according to some beliefs, eating animals (excluding human species) is important to keep the animal population in check, then is human slaughter not important to keep the population of human animal in check and also in prevention of destruction to natural habitats?? A restriction or imposition of beliefs should thus be unbiased and in accordance with the laws of nature that serves to balance the population load of all species in nature.

We often believe that eating meat or killing an animal for flesh is a sin and the person who is doing that will go to hell and will even face the punishment in his life. Well even in the past rich were having a lavish life, with fine booze and rich animal diet but they progressed at the same time. They enjoyed most of royal luxury and still do. A common man cannot afford these and is only surviving on the grains while leading a life of struggle and poverty.

Most of us ignore the unpopular fact that plants are also living beings. They too reproduce, consume food and even excrete like we do. But their immobility renders them helpless in the hands of destiny. They can be burnt, chopped and even treated with dangerous pesticides mercilessly and they cannot rebel, cry in pain or express sorrow or remorse. Due to this lack of animal/human – like sensation or emotion or blood, they are frequently considered as non-living and are mercilessly killed for food, paper, furniture, and all other human needs. There are unlimited benefits of killing plants and animals and they do tend to provide utility for us. If you go through an ancient scripture or a religious book, you will find the instances where Gods are frequently portrayed wearing animal skin, animal bones and are even known to kill giant animals like crocodiles, horses, and deers under the excuse of stories or mythological explanations justifying the slaughter.

Is animal slaughter in the hands of God a justified theory? We have a tendency to develop a blind faith in whatever we are taught by the fake gurus and in case of logical doubt we are considered as atheist. It has been seen that noshing excessive meat mostly leads to increased cholesterol and ultimately leads to a death via heart attack and high blood pressure or similar cholesterol related diseases. A blind orthodox mindset usually considers it a punishment of his sin but from the doctor's point of view, he died due to high cholesterol or high protein intake. So, everyone has their own set of explanations for their actions.

Today we cannot imagine our life without leather, from shoes to belts to brief cases to even car seats we need leather, have any guru tried to create a campaign against leather on large scale? Has anyone stood for bulls that are mercilessly killed for skin and I have never seen any fish rights organisation standing for fish rights.

The thing is we humans have made adjustments according to our needs and we know how to give reasons for our acts. There are places where local food is not available especially in case of forest inhabitants; they are compelled to kill for food as well as for self guard. Similarly, animals are eating other animals for survival. Don't you think human is the biggest animal of the world who is not only eating other animals but also using them according to the operations specified.

You must have heard about the theory, the man who eats like a cow or an elephant is fat and the one who eat like a tiger is muscular and athletic. The reason behind this lies in the nutrients, proteins and vitamins he gets from the food which helps his body in maintenance and growth. The one who is eating the tiger is defiantly having a rich source of protein which aids in muscle building and strong bones but the one who is consuming grains or rice is only having rich carbohydrates which are simple sugars resulting to excessive fat. Again we can even get all the nutrients from vegan diet too.

I don't advocate you to start eating meat or any animal. It all depends on your beliefs and choice. Some don't eat meat with this fact that the one who is killed is an animal and the process of killing animal is obviously brutal. Even the animal eaters cannot stand the abattoir for 5 minutes since it becomes difficult to witness the brutal killing of animal in front of them.

Besides consumption, there is one more reason for which we kill animals or any other creature and that is for our safe guard. Almost everyone in this world uses rat killers, mosquito repellents, fly trap and cockroach killer hit to remove them from our home. We don't have any other alternative except killing them which we justify in the name of safe guard. If we will not kill them they will give us various kinds of diseases. So it's not necessary that you are killing creatures for food there are countless reasons. And it is impossible to cover and exempt yourself from this. I guess these gurus must be having good solution to the issue of insects and rats.

Talking about liquor it is equally in bad reputation as meat. When it is used in medicine and syrups it creates wonders and when consumed directly it creates liver damage and many other common diseases which alcoholics face. Generally woman don't like it as the man whom they are kissing is spitting out awful smell but with every new day the liquor consumers are increasing as the effect after inhaling the same is outstanding. It is not important to be a non vegetarian to become a drinker and again there is no spiritual connection to it. From the past kings and queens are known for their leisure which constitute liquor of course and the extreme methods of worship do involve liquor offering in some religious practises but still no sacred book or no god or goddess has asked for liquor or meat straight away.

In reality there are so many objectionable things humans do which are normal for some community and taboo for some, the thing is we have to live with them as we live with diverse creatures together if we want peace and harmony in kalyug.

16
ARE WELL WISHERS AND ENEMIES SENT BY GOD?

The world is filled with various creatures and species and among them the human species are the most abundant. We all are connected to each other by various means. The most common way is through relatives, friends, acquaintances and work mates. Besides connecting to the known people we also get connected to strangers who cross our path in the form of friends or enemies. Human is a social animal and cannot survive alone; we need people around us in different roles who facilitate our life physically, emotionally and mentally. To reach a position in life we take help and support from every person surrounding us. Similarly, everyone has similar dreams and aspirations to lead a successful life and in the quest for the same we do not hesitate to use each other for money, luxury and fame.

In order to know and understand things and in order to work we often meet people outside our comfort zone. The experience we had with the stranger determines the definition of an enemy or friend for us at the end of the day. We often blame God for the betrayal we get and sometimes also thank God when we are saved from a grave danger.

But is God really sending them to us? Or is it the karma of some deed? The reality is that every creature of this world is cheated as well as helped and this theory is not spiritual but practical and logical. Almost every country has similar difficulties as well as similar crimes affecting the billions. The difference is only slight, ranging from types of crimes to its frequency of occurrence. People die and their family suffers, no matter which culture they belong to. Just like ups and downs are a common thing people face, getting friends and fiends is too. The universal law that applies here is the survival of the fittest.

It would be foolish to say that the divine deity, the supreme almighty plans barriers and enemies in our lives. Even he is himself known to have faced betrayal as well as friendships when he incarnated on Earth. So, the God cannot be the guilty one for our bad experiences or bad fate since our experiences hugely depend on our reaction to things. If we are good for millions and we can be bad for billions. Everything is fair in our struggle to survive.

If a person is deeply spiritual he may hesitate in stealing your money but a non-believer may rob you completely. Nobody has time to think about good or bad or the consequences today.

When we are betrayed, we end up in a state of non belief and when something good happens our beliefs are reinstated. Some people believe in the presence of God and consider everyone as the gift of God but the world is a big

Jungle of animals fighting for their survival. We are met with new dangers each day, each time and we react according to our nature and experience. Thinking about innocent animals that are beaten, tortured, murdered and even eaten alive by humans, the helpless beings don't even have the option to question "Are these well wishers and enemies sent by God?"

17
PEOPLE ARE GETTING AWAY FROM GOD AS THEY ARE GETTING URBANISED

There are many gurus who have started a war against science and urbanisation. They hate the fact that things are changing very rapidly and the change is not only physical but personal as well. From the conservative attire to the open discussions on topics like sexuality and gay pride, everything is changing. The women who were destined to a life of domestic violence are now seeking freedom from the marriage imprisonment; the population that was tolerating the corruption of the politicians are now raising voice against the same.

Things are changing very rapidly and this change is an issue for the people still living with an orthodox thinking. There are countless gurus and political leaders who still carry an orthodox thinking. They still advocate the life of women in the veil. They still consider homosexuality as a disease. They still believe in specific submissive role of woman to be a housewife in day and a courtesan at night and they still want the common people to behave deaf, blind and dumb. Since they are losing their ages old authority, they take the help of spirituality to bring people back to their social status.

They believe that by creating the fear of God they will be able to prevent the people from social advancements. It is easy to fool the ones who are illiterate and ignorant towards advancements and spiritual awakening and if we add poverty with illiteracy, it is easy to create an animal out of a human. Yes! The people who are weak in terms of education and money are often treated and used as animals. The quest for survival and the absence of money and knowledge makes them dumb, deaf and blind. The same easily makes them a puppet in the hands of the gurus and politicians. And the politicians also play a major role towards such situation by raising tax rates, inflation in every commodity, violence in the name of religion, ambience of emergency, revolts and the list is endless. The struggles to fulfil daily needs of food, clothing and shelter lands such people in a fear of survival and at last compels them to take shelter under religion, God and the remedies by Gurus who further exploit them to their advantage.

God never asked you to avoid technology or advancement. In fact, it is the gift of science that we are living a better life in human body. In absence of technology and advancement the human living will return to Stone Age or maybe even resemble that of animals. Inventions have not only created the history but also changed the lifestyle, ideology and behaviour of the masses.

The more the advancement, the more will be the understanding of reality as well as spirituality. Mental and technological advancements will enable human species to excel in the spheres of knowledge and also to be able to differentiate between the reality and spirituality. They will be able to detect the fake myths and take better decisions in the course of life which will further contribute to the betterment of the living. It is very important to walk past the orthodox ideologies and be urbanised and advanced in the age of kalyug.

18
MATERIAL LUST

Has anybody ever told you that your material lust or love for assets is keeping you away from God? Well! It may sound familiar to you if you are a regular visitor of the gurus. Most of the gurus advocate that material lust or money or luxuries are the elements which are keeping us away from God. This is highly absurd and illogical statement I have heard many times by almost every guru.

They pretend to negate it so much, as if, they literally never use any luxury or thing of material value.

I know material lust and the greed for money leads to crime and corruption and that is a universal fact but is it possible to live without assets, money and materials that facilitate our lives and give us a better world?

The gurus advocate us a life where we chant carols of God 24X7 and not do anything at all. They say that this advancement and urbanisation is dangerous. They contend that we are dead spiritually as we have become the meanest and the most competitive personnel in life. Although, I agree to the argument that we are dead spiritually; I do not agree with urbanisation being as dangerous for us as it is projected to be. Since ages evolution has created better mutated genes eliminating what is obsolete or no longer useful. We as a species and part of Mother Nature have done similar with civilizing and urbanizing ourselves. Like the mutated genes, we live in a mutated world, a mutated civilization that keeps improving, eliminating what is obsolete and no longer useful. Just like mutations bring with it both good and bad alleles, the urbanization brings with it both good and bad consequences (Pollution for example is a bad consequence of machines). The overall emphasis of evolution is the preservation of those who have the best probability for survival and in the process it keeps improving, for the survival of the fittest. Similarly, the overall emphasis of the urbanization is to mutate a society that contributes to the better working of human race (advent of vaccines and medications improving mortality rate, advancement of food and cooking from raw grains and leaves to baked bread and cooked veggies, clothes from leaves to woven fabric, caves to homes with many facilities like modern bed as compared to the pile of dried leaves, advent of better means of communication, and many more.)

We dramatise our love for God but in reality we have true love for assets and property only. To understand this fact, we need not argue over the human species only. The observations of the animal kingdom brings to us natural characters where creatures mark their territories by their smell or urine, fight for authority of their clan, make families, build specialised nests or burrows, conspire and hunt together to bring down a large enemy, court the female for making love and also fight over their women of course. The animals may not be having any barter system or money exchanges but they do tend to fight on the issues of area, boundaries and females. They do not dramatise the practise of God which humans do.

Logically, it is impossible for a person to leave everything aside and worship God 24x7. In this kalyug, Miracles do not feed us. To fill our stomach we must work hard ourselves. Even the gurus who have been befooling people in the name of God are now trying hard to find out other passive jobs for survival and with the same attempt they frequently set up parallel businesses or worship houses as source of income via sales and donations. Even in animal world, an animal has to catch a pray to foster his hunger or feed on the grass else he will die. The body which is created by the God requires food and comforts for its survival.

According to many gurus, you should live a saintly life, away from luxury and comforts depending upon satvik diet (food/fruits uncooked or that fallen naturally from trees) and worshipping God continuously for all hours for all life. But according to that criterion, in today's reality the authenticity of the saints is also in question

Talking about materialistic comforts, luxury, assets, need and desire, according to mythological tales even the God has enjoyed and leisured these materialistic assets and luxuries when he incarnated himself on the earth and this is evident in many mythological scripts and tales cited by religious gurus in their religious and spiritual teachings. Besides assets the Gods had beautiful houses, extraordinary ornaments and vehicles like flying machines. Many of these are material assets and the mythological tales that present such rich and luxurious life of Gods also cite material lust as the reason behind battles and wars where Gods are known to fight the bad ones for assets, land, territories and even for women.

Such stories eloquently indicate that even the Gods were not able to leave these assets and luxuries when they incarnated themselves on earth. So the statements by gurus asking to desist from materialistic leisure are again in question.

A person cannot live a life without working and it's obvious that hard work gives reward. So if a man works a little he is able to get food and if the same man works harder he gets food and shelter but when he crosses the extreme stage of his usual hard work he gets rewarded with food and shelter but in the most upgraded way. You may sleep on the floor or may sleep on a couch, the difference is of the asset you are using but on either of these you are doing the same job and that is sleeping. Similarly, from a saint to a labour to a business man, everybody worships one almighty God and God listens to all of them, no matter what their profession is.

Most of the gurus who fail to attract much limelight or in other terms are out of work in their so called spiritual profession advocate these statements of sacrifice and retirement. They know enormous success is hard to achieve and one cannot endure himself or prosper without hard work or reward. The people will eventually find it difficult and will surrender in front of the guru for shortcuts or miraculous remedies. On the other hand, the famous gurus who live in big bungalows, travel in luxury sedans and make frequent foreign visits are also advocating the same statements besides the fact that they are using and enjoying these materialistic leisures more than any common man.

Some gurus say that man is a fool who is after science trying to re-discover the things already written in ancient scriptures. Some advocate that the mortal life won't last forever, so the quest to earn and struggle is useless, instead a life should be spent in worshipping all the time. They forget the technologies enable them to connect with foreign lands and preach their baseless teachings. All these discoveries need physical hard work.

Human discoveries and hard work has changed the life of billions and these gurus also come in the category of enjoyers like any common person who is enjoying the creations of human kind. The fact is that as urbanisation and technology is crossing its height people are becoming more logical and practical. This practicality is questioning the orthodox practices and superstition, the two words on which the entire foundation of the business of these gurus exist.

Excess of everything is bad and this also applies to material and money. But the importance of these assets in our life cannot be denied as well. It's better to advocate tolerance, forgiveness, humanity and realisation instead of advocating complete boycott of all the material leisure created by human's hard work. A human can incorporate tolerance, forgiveness and humanity besides enjoying the material assets and luxuries and also awaken himself spiritually to reach the divine in this Kalyug.

19
A WOMAN – AN IMPURITY

A woman being not allowed to enter most of the worship places is more due to the fact that they are considered an impurity and less due to being a weaker sex. The basic formation and working of a female body becomes the reason for the same. They say 'A deity or God being considered a purest form of divine, must not be touched by anything that is impure'. That is why every place is cleaned before worshipping so as to eliminate the presence of anything evil or impure. And the same becomes the reason for such a discriminatory treatment towards the female sex especially at the time of pregnancy or menstruation.

The label of 'Impure Sex' is so widespread that almost all major religions in the world have rituals for women purification and most of them are conducted during or after menstruation or childbirth. And till the time the woman is 'Impure', she is not allowed to enter any worship houses. In some cultures, a woman during menstruation cannot touch an idol of god and cannot even enter the kitchen (which is considered a place of purity), while in some others they are sent to live outside the village too. Only after the 'days of impurity' are over, she is allowed to come back or carry on life at a normal pace. Some cultures also attribute nature's call and physical love making a thing of impurity, after which one must not enter the worship houses or touch anything related to God. But some religions have crossed the lines of extremity by completely abandoning women from entering the worship houses or even worshipping a particular deity.

There are also rituals and temples where gods of fertility and the male reproductive organs are worshipped (Phallic worship) as a sign of fertility and life. Why is then a woman, who is the pivotal element in giving life to a creature labelled with a tag completely opposite to the Godly image of the male reproductive organ?? Such gender discrimination not only demeans the status of woman in society but also gives air to crimes against women. The situation is worsened when the elderly females or females with an orthodox thinking support such gender discrimination. Owing to the same discriminatory social beliefs and practises the concept of Casanova becomes a matter of pride whereas the female having more than one sexual partner is frequently labelled as a sex worker.

These are not the only discriminatory rituals that exist. There have been times when if a man died, his wife was accused of being unlucky or even the witch who devoured her husband. The question that stands here is 'WHY IS A WOMAN CONSIDERED A THING OF IMPURITY FOR SOMETHING THAT IS NATURAL TO HER EXISTENCE AND IS THE MOST IMPORTANT FACTOR IN THE

BIRTH OF A LIFE?'

It is a fact well established that on the entire planet, except sea horse, only female species is capable of giving birth but unlike mammals or humans in particular, the status of female counterparts is generally at dominance in a relationship and/or in society (Matriarchal societies). In animal species (Like Polar bears) the females are courted by the potential male counterparts. The males of the species initiate a courtship display prior to love making so as to present himself as the perfect suitor. For this, they commonly display their power in a combat with another male so as to establish a high rank which further contributes to their reproductive success and increases chances of mating with more females. In some other species (like peacock spiders and humming birds) the males display a variety of abilities and talents so as to be the chosen one. In species like Lions, Elephants, Bees, Ants, Killer whales and even Bonobo apes, female dominance in the society marks the Matriarchal society. Worth noting here is that the Bonobo apes are among the nearest relatives of Human species. Hence, according to the laws of nature, the female counterpart of a species play an upper hand, most of the time. But it is not exactly the case in human species where the Males are worshipped as deities while the status of women is much lower or even stands at the label of impurity.

The cultural disbeliefs along with famous statements that are known to be preached by the gurus and Gods further add to worsening the status of women in the society when they are misinterpreted and preached in the misinterpreted form. Such misinterpreted phrases or sayings rendering violence justified are frequently attached with religion or teachings from scriptures by religious gurus where some even preach that the drum, the poor, the animals and the women, should be beaten to get the best out of them. When such wrongly interpreted phrases are adopted as the ideal culture or conduct in the society, they render the discrimination and crimes against women as rightly justified. In such cases it has been observed that even the parents ask their daughter to adjust than to revolt, when she is faced with domestic violence by her husband. Similar notions also become basis for crimes against women, including but not limited to rapes, marital rapes, female infanticides, prostitution, female trafficking, etc.

In many cultures the male is worshipped and treated like deity. Even the younger male child is given the priority over the elder female child. Many cultures over the time have developed a set of rules or codes of conduct to raise an ideal girl to be an ideal women and the codes usually include the teachings of servitude towards the husband and in-laws, to never speak when the man is speaking, a woman's voice should always be low, the female must always be obedient, she must always eat at last, sleep at last and rise up at the earliest. Some cultures also advocate a compulsory practise of veil and the females who are quite liberal in mannerisms or in conversations with males are often considered of a low character and sometimes equivalent to sex workers which further gives rise to crimes like gang rapes or corrective rapes where punishing an impudent woman by raping her is rendered justified by many members of the society. It is a matter of no wonder that a female even with a slight rumour of getting engaged in romantic relationships with a man prior to marriage loses her tag of being a good, ideal, obedient girl and the social trend now-a-days is therefore moving towards portrayal of ideal feminism to fetch good suitors.

But many notions are not what they seem like. If we go through various sacred scriptures, we will find that gender discrimination is not supported in sacred religious books and they seem more of originated via tell tales, misinterpreted religious texts, misleading teaching by religious mentors and society over a huge span of time.

The cultural and religious practices today are quite contrary to the teachings originally mentioned in the sacred books that attribute equal status for both men and women and advocates no gender discrimination between a man and woman and further states that both man and woman are equal in the eyes of the supreme divine. [Holy Quran Verse 3:195, Galatians 3:28-29 , 1 Corinthians 11:12 , Genesis 1:27 and 5:1-2, Rig veda 2-17-16, Rig veda 10-27-12, Rig veda 12-2-31]

20
WHY PEOPLE WORSHIP GOD IN KALYUG?

In every house and in every religion, there is usually a tradition to worship God in the morning. This activity is mainly allowed to those who are clean by body and pray for the cleanliness of soul. Therefore, many cultures insist upon having a bath before entering worship house or even touching a sacred book. However, many advocate this to be unnecessary since a clean soul matters more than a clean body, arguing that a clean body is of no importance if the soul is ridden with bad deeds or sins.

And so for worshipping there are worship houses where people can pray, meditate or chant carols in the name of God, where the latter is perceived either in the form of stone idols, or as shrines, or as an imaginary figure. Worshipping is done in every religion in almost the same manner. Every religion has songs in the praise of God which they chant and sing, praising the God for his mercy, for his qualities, stories of good deeds, stories of courage that not only gives us strength but also hope, courage and confidence that their holy father will protect us from difficulties, give them strength to face struggles, show them the right path and will also rescue them from problems. The act of praying magically provides such a comfort that even a wrong doer prays to God for safety and safe escape. We are well aware that God is Omnipresent, Omniscient, and Omnipotent and that we stand with a naked soul in front of God but we still try to fool him sometimes by fake or perceived victimisation claiming us to be in trouble because of others. We know what we did and we also realise our mistakes and its consequences, but our ego ignores the point of realisation

We believe that worshiping God will erase our past and this belief is injected into our brains by the gurus. You can purchase commodities and goods via money but you cannot purchase the medicine for the removal of the marks of your bad deeds since the impact of injury is high that tends to affect us as well as the ones harmed by us.

Some argue that visiting the worship houses famous for the divine miracles, bathing in the sacred rivers or things like fasts, will purify our soul but this also looks more like another blind belief since if this theory really works then every rapist, terrorist or murderer will erase their brutal sins via showers, fasts and pilgrimages and will attain salvation.

The reality is that the excessive human lust has degraded for us the value of everything we have today, be it a temple or a river or even God. The monuments and worship houses known for their outstanding past are now used as an income source by the political leaders and fake gurus. In some worship homes even the feast of God is available on paid basis. In other words in kalyug you have to pay for even visiting your almighty. This is such a irony that the creator who has provided everything free to us, is now available on paid basis, by the humans for the humans, but the question worth asking here is that the worship houses are really homes of Almighty or are just business houses opened in the name of God?. So, in simple words it is just another business but the faith and fear is so strong that raising voice against this also seems scary to many.

Many of us are so psychologically mind washed about the effect of worship homes that half of our problems are resolved in our minds and if by chance a coincidence happens like our prayers become a reality, we consider that to be the power of worship homes and God. Everyone has a different faith according to their belief, but the world progresses, people succeed in their ventures whether they follow any religion, any God and even when they are atheists. Every creature of this planet is entitled to food and survival and it depends on him how he makes his journey to life. From humans to animals to mammal to insects every creature is given full liberty and endless resources to explore and live. The animals never worship God and they don't even have a religion for living but they are still getting food and life.

God has never asked you worship him to gain monetary benefits in return in fact he has allowed us a free life to live and work. We get the opportunities in life but it depends on us whether to do something great or do something useless. He has provided us with plenty of resources and above that an amazing body and extraordinary mind which can even make us the king of this world but the absolute owner will still be God.

21
WHY PEOPLE HATE GOD IN KALYUG?

The concept of God is so vast that almost entire life will be spent and we will still be reading the first chapter. It is a divine concept and the more we try to understand the more we end up in mystery because it is impossible to know God and so, many of us perceive God in various forms. The life we got is exceptional, yet not an easy one. The day to day struggles for survival are increasing so rapidly that it becomes hard to carry on when our patience is always running out. We feel so much stressed and pressurised in our daily lives that everything happening to and around us seems unfair. We meet wrong people every now and then. Everyone seems ready to nosh us alive and we feel helpless in protecting ourselves. Moreover, besides our countless prayers and remedies for a better life, we end up being more exhausted which provokes us sometimes to question the existence of God in kalyug.

We pray to God millions of times but we hear nothing in return. The people who are embarrassing humanity by their acts are prospering while the victims are being punished mercilessly. The zenith of unfairness and unethical activities is scattered altogether everywhere. When unfavourable time knocks someone's door, things work against the person and he cannot determine what he should do. At the time, the person lands up in an emotionally and mentally pathetic state.

Ignorance from God provokes him badly and he starts questioning the role of God in his life. He demands favours in return for the worships he has been doing so far. He asks for the price of his devotion in terms of help but when even this doesn't work, his anger ignites up towards the almighty. He decides to hate God or disobey the teachings he had learnt, since they are rendered useless and not workable. All that he had learnt about God does not seem to be happening in the real life. Most of us have learnt that God punishes the demon and is there to help people every time they need him. He is omnipresent and is watching over everyone while giving the right fruit according to the activities people are doing.

But when the same person gets harmed or destroyed and the destroyer does not even get a fragment of bruise, the devotee feels cheated as well as misguided. His positivity goes into the dustbin and the negative energies surround him. He starts hating the world as well as the people. He even develops hatred for the ones who are happy and in some cases such hatred is also expressed through violence either on animals or on humans. Other's pains give him a sadistic relief and he enjoys watching people cry as he also cried at some point in life, he was also wronged sometime and there was no one to help him, not even God, so the bitterness turns him turned into the aggressor and he never feels the need to have emotions or even pain.

The people who develop hatred towards God tend to

hate everything created by God. Besides hating themselves, they develop hatred towards life, all the living creatures and the worse they do the more they enjoy. There condition is like an irritated child who destroys everything in the house to express his anger. In case of annoyed humans this condition is more severe than it appears. They become so sure of the absence of God that they challenge him by doing the evilest works.

There are millions out there who are against God or label themselves as non-believer or atheists and the reason for that are the obstacles and hindrances they have faced on every step of their life. Each time they sought God, they were disappointed and so the human by virtue of its natural tendency to observe, test, analyse and infer, infers that God does not exist. Besides hating God such people sometimes resort towards evil powers and demons through black magic. The negative atmosphere created around their life dominates them so badly that they spend their entire life in planning things against humanity.

Example of anti-God activities can be taken from terrorist activities. Most of the terrorists and terrorist groups are not true devotees or worshipers of their religion or God. In fact, they are against God, love, brotherhood as well as humanity. They use the term God to fetch an army of innocent youngsters to implement their destructive revenges. They brainwash the youngsters so nicely that each of them lose their ability of thinking and decision making. The main objective of their life becomes destruction of human kind. It is more like an open war.

It was believed that only illiterate people are prone towards such thinking but in past few years reality has surfaced when more educated numbers came forward as master minds behind some major tragedies in history of the World. You cannot predict who is against humanity and who is not. Hence, the world is dangerous because every person is living according to their own beliefs.

When we see a criminal getting sentenced, we generally say that he got the punishment of his bad deeds while the same criminal believes that he has been caught due to some mistake or carelessness. He goes to jail and again starts figuring out the ways of escape and further implementation of the crime but this time with greater caution.

Some people start hating God when their loved one dies. They believe that God has taken away their loved one and hence ruined their life. The emptiness becomes difficult to cope up with and God is looked upon as guilty since there was no miracle away from the God's wand, yet he chose that pain for them, that too when they worshipped him from all their heart and soul. Such brutality is unforgivable and as a punishment to God, people tend to boycott him or even develop bitter hatred towards the same.

It is well learnt that all that is born is destined to end; all that rises is destined to set. Nothing in the world is immortal. But even after knowing facts, our mind is tangled in the created conviction that miracles happen and God makes them happen. A major contribution to such thinking comes from the teachings of gurus who, by their fictional and mythological stories, create a belief that with the power of prayers and belief even the dead can be raised to life. We expect God to protect us, fulfil all our wishes and also raise our loved ones to life but this does not happen in kalyug and hence, the hatred is but natural.

Scientifically speaking, human or Homo sapiens is the highest form of animal in the animal kingdom and like other species is subject to the laws of Nature where the quest for survival and the survival of the fittest go hand in hand. The one who is eaten is called as pray and the one who eats is called as stalker. Each species is equipped with tools to defend itself as well as with tools to attack. Human today needs to understand this simple concept of survival and lead himself towards spiritual awakening.

Although, there is no reason to hate God but god will be loved by many and hated by many. Like the two sides of a coin, there exists 'good God' and 'bad God' in kalyug.

22
WHY PEOPLE NEED GURUS, WORSHIP INSTITUTES AND RELIGIOUS MONUMENTS?

People need gurus as well as worship houses just like we need food in our life; in other words for survival. In the absence of the same, life will become an endless nightmare and the world will become a war zone. You must be thinking that this chapter seems contrary to all other chapters that mention the ill practises and fake actions of the gurus violating the ideology of the masses and also raises objection on blind beliefs, superstitious notions and baseless practises that people perform in their daily lives. The reason behind that is not a past tradition which should be maintained nor it is an attempt to justify some religion. The main reason of advocating that is to preserve some fragments of humanity.

In reality humans are among the most inhuman species in the world and the reason lies in their actions and living. Human species have been so powerful since history that they made infinite changes to the environment for self leisure and needs. There was a time when nature and animals were only the sufferers in the hands of human torture but today humans are killing and competing with fellow human as well, just like any other animal survival race. Cannibalism here need not follow the basic definition of noshing meat of own species. Humans are devouring each other by various other means. The practises of crime, corruption, betrayal, murder, rape are not less than killing.

A question pops as to what is the role of any guru or worship houses in this? No matter how much the fake gurus lead the people astray, there are still spiritual mentors who provide knowledge, truth and awakening. They may not be very popular but are certainly rich in knowledge. They may not be enjoying the silver thrones but certainly do enjoy the dedication towards the supreme divine.

Talking about silver thrones, many spiritual mentors as well as their followers argue that they hold the right to live a happy materialistic life and that their spiritual teachings are like the services provided to the common man. Like doctors and lawyers sell their time to us, gurus do the same, and the difference is only in the service they are offering. For a living, money is a requirement and if a business of spirituality turns out to be one of the most lucrative business, then how are they at fault in this? Some also argue that this profession is among the hardest professions in the world since one has to sit back the entire day giving teachings and attending a huge population for the remedies to their problems. Anything like this, if done without any money will soon challenge their survival and no wonder might also lead to death via starvation or subject them to a life of beggary and misery. Since now-a-days almost everyone enjoys a married life, they also have certain responsibilities towards their families that can't be met unless they charge for their teachings or start parallel businesses of religious teachings or products relating to worshipping.

The pivotal aspect worthy of consideration while availing the services of these religious service providers is the quality of their services or the quality of their teachings. Any teaching that contributes towards a derogatory society or towards creating differences among humans or tends to inflict emotional, moral, societal or humanistic harm directly or indirectly, should never be preferred as a quality spiritual teaching. If the spiritual teaching is good and is a spiritual teaching in true sense, concentrating more towards spiritual awakening, then I believe supporting such an institution monetarily will only serve to do good for the mankind and hence should be supported. Otherwise too, expecting a system to be selfless in Kalyug is like travelling to moon on foot.

It has been seen that people need someone to motivate them. They look out for god in human form who will come and work out all the issues of their life. It is generally observed that many fake gurus, at the start of their carrier, teach such wonderful spiritual insights that you will end up divinifying them. The problem starts when we see their real side, the ugly side which is ridden with crimes, indecent activities or even surplus avarice and corruption. Regarding a life of leisure, one might argue that it is no wrong. But when it's a question of a spiritual guru, people tend to carry a preformed image in their minds that is acquired mostly from the mythological tales. It is the same image, nature, character, feature and even the attire and celibacy that people expect from their ideal spiritual guru. The ones not conforming to this image are often criticized for two reasons: (1) for not following the idealism according to scriptures; (2) their avarice, corruption and similar actions signal contradiction to their own teachings.

I believe in such circumstances, the professional tag of a 'Motivational Speaker' is more appropriate than the tag of a spiritual guru since the former allows the spiritual mentors to maintain their lifestyle more comfortably.

People need a guru to guide them, to make a positive change in their lives and to help them remain motivated towards life. When life offers difficulties people seek God and when God is not present they seek the incarnated soul which they find in the gurus and in the worship houses. The gurus who impart good knowledge and good teachings create a sense of patience and satisfaction in people and no matter what religion they belong to, they will surely have faith in God which in turn gives them the motivational energy to face any struggle.

      Similarly, visiting worship houses imparts a sense of psychological relief and strength to humans which makes them believe that God is still there and no matter what comes in life almighty will help them in all walks of life. Another common belief associated with visiting worship houses is the notion that God resides at worship houses more than anywhere else in the world, and thus by performing religious ceremonies, God can be compelled to come down on Earth and reside in stone idols and tombs. This belief motivates them to keep hoping that someday like they will reach God, they will attain salvation as well.

      Since these stone idols or religious monuments are constructed out of materialistic assets, expecting Godly justice from stone idols will seem more of foolishness than a miracle. But this does have a potent effect on people who get filled with enormous hope and motivation via the same stone idols. You can call it a placebo effect. It is not necessary to get justice by stone idols but it makes people believe in a judgement day when all wrong/evil will be punished and all good will be rewarded or maybe even given salvation. It keeps the people realised that someone is watching over them every time and one must do good to have good done to them. But it is also seen that people make their own definitions of God and justify their actions by manipulating the verdicts written in mythological scriptures like a person who kills someone who has encroached his property believes that his act is religiously justified for squashing the bad and hence it is the victory of good over bad.

      Thus, it proves that People cannot live without Gods , their religious monuments and their messengers known as gurus because in absence of the same people will treat themselves as God and will eventually kill whomsoever comes in the way considering it as the God's verdict in kalyug.

23
THE MYSTERY OF ALIENS IN KALYUG

We have always been fascinated by the word alien and we are always eager to know about them. The mystery and our fascination for them excites us and provokes us to know more about them.

Almost every culture or religion has talked about aliens and Gods in their manuscripts. You may search any part of the world; you will get to hear some ancient cases of aliens and Gods that are presented with facts and evidences supporting those claims. Not just that, the field of science is also active in researching these avenues.

Almost every culture or religion has mythological tales and scriptures that iterate stories about Gods, Goddesses, Demons, Angels and Spirits who incarnated on Earth for a special purpose and most of them are known to be associated with animals and known to arrive on chariots, flying machines, flying animals, and some even appeared out from the Earth itself. Almost every culture or mythological tale has descriptions of their Gods in these forms. Besides having technologically advanced vehicles, they were different in personality, looks and even appearance. Some were simply wrapped in a white cloth and some were grandly decorated with jewels or carried different weapons and instruments. Thinkers argue that if they were God then why they needed machines to travel from Heaven or Hell to the Earth? The creator does not need any vehicle to travel if he is a divine spirit and the creator of the universe. They are also carrying weapons and instruments. The overall analysis hints that they were similar to today's astronauts. To reach a planet today we need rockets which are today's flying machines, specialised instruments as well as weapons for safety because we never know what we will be facing on a planet that is completely alien to us.

Secondly, if we even assume that those who visited our ancestors in ancient times were Gods and not aliens, then also, this statement is contradictory raising doubt as to why God needed to change their name and appearance according to different religions? If every religion has different Gods then their section of the Universe, Heaven, Hell, Earth and other planets must also be divided according to their rights, as we do here on earth. So this apparently indicates that the people who visited Earth in ancient times, in flying machines, could have been aliens or other extraterrestrial beings that are today called as Gods.

The scientists today also advocate this theory. If we talk about universe, according to the Big Bang theory scientists believed that there are uncountable worm holes in the universe which are used by the aliens and other creatures to travel to Earth. In almost every scripture you can find the stories and instances that mention of spirits or God or a powerful energy coming through a portal or a star gate but according to science those portals are nothing but are wormholes which are perfect medium for travelling from one planet to another.

Our scriptures also talk about heaven and hell and some scriptures state that hell is inside the earth and heaven is above the sky and that the Gods came from heaven above the sky and demons came from hell situated below the ground. This also supports the theory of aliens raising a possibility that the aliens who helped our ancestors were considered Devta or Gods and the ones who troubled our ancestors were defined as demons by our ancestors. The similarity between the Gods and the humans in terms of behaviour, lifestyle and wars indicates a common link between the two and reflects upon the accuracy of the alien theory. Gods do not need to fight with a demon or a human for woman, land, pride, power or anything materialistic which becomes an ignored fact contrary to the tales in sacred scriptures. Fighting for territory, possessions, partner or other things have always been the traits attributed to species. Aliens are nothing but some species living on a different planet. It can thus be concluded that Gods who descended on Earth were actually aliens coming from other planet.

All around the world amazing monoliths and monuments have been found which are exceptional as well as incredible from the architectural point of view. Besides having the best engineering techniques and machines it feels impossible to construct such monoliths today but the people of the ancient world still created the things of wonder without having any such technology as we have today. An astonishing finding is that all these monolithic monuments are precise in terms of calculation, geometry and even appearance. It is believed that besides being large they are also exhibiting a message or even a mysterious code. Some monuments are hard to understand and it seems unnecessary today to construct such giant structures but their construction by the people in ancient times raises a thought provoking doubt as to what was the need to construct such big monolithic sculptures? Why did our ancestors construct monoliths? And how did they do it? Can a man construct something extraordinary without any specialised tools or machinery? I guess not. But yes it is a possibility that they were helped by some extraterrestrial force or beings who could have helped in the making of these structures. Searching through the mythological scriptures, tales about Gods coming to Earth and helping man in construction of huge structures are also found. Does that again provide a connecting link between Gods and aliens?

Moreover, it has been seen that almost all cultures have tales of Gods and Demons inscribed on stones, which can be a large piece of stone finely carved or a monolith or even a mountain. But an amazing observation is that such stony inscriptions are common in all cultures and countries. But why is this similarity widespread? It can be a possibility that humans were ordered to do this either by gods or by an aliens. They were also aware about the fact that stone does not degrade unlike other metals and minerals and their choice of stone as a medium also depicts a fact that this attempt of crafting the stone idols, scriptures and monoliths was done to give knowledge to the coming generation. it is also believed that these monoliths are not merely a piece of stone which depict the deity and the god but they also gather a certain amount of power and energy source which was used by gods, aliens and even ancient humans. But if we try to match it with today's craftsmanship of temples and monuments, they are build with same old pattern of bricks and mortar and does not carry any mysterious technology which cannot be understood by humans. The gods sculptures made out of stone today are losing their credibility in kalyug as they are made with the intention of money and not as a medium of spiritual paranormal connection.

A surprising finding is that most of the monoliths and monuments were made in specific order that resembled the pattern of the solar system, the planets, the stars as well as the life. Even the megalithic landscapes are made different and it is believed that the main reason of building them was to highlight them as a different platform to connect to the spiritual and alien world.

In mythological tales, we have also read about Gods coming to Earth in their flying machines and visiting people at the time of celebrations. But does God really need a machine to travel? Can it be a possibility that the ones who came to Earth were aliens from another planet just like we go to mars and moon? It is also stated in many sacred scriptures that in ancient times, there lived people who were half human and half animal. They were equipped with special powers. The scriptures also mention of humans that were born with extraordinary magical powers. But then where are all powers gone in the modern today? It is impossible to digest both facts as truths, and if we consider one of them as a true fact then the other one highly becomes fictitious. We have also read that there were talking animals who could speak in human tongue and humans were not only equipped in flying but also equipped in disappearing as well as changing the gender. But if this is not possible, then it raises doubts on the authenticity of the mythological scriptures and if that was possible then explanation of today's powerless man becomes difficult. But there can be a possibility of yet another kind of highly mutated species that had a half man half animal body or was well versed in human tongue. The possibility of another kind of highly mutated species fits perfectly with aliens. It can also be a possibility that the aliens helped humans in fighting with the demons or another group of aliens and also guided them with right knowledge and education.

    A lot of monuments today are considered haunted as well as sacred. They are not only marked as haunted but are also allowed visitors for some restricted hours by the archaeological survey. Such monuments are marked high on the scale of paranormal activity and are considered unsafe at night. In some Indian temples, it is also a famous belief that Gods descend there during night and kill the spectators (if any), to prevent their mystery from being divulged to the world. If it is a ghost, then it can be detected by paranormal devices or trapped by priests but if it is God then it becomes impossible to believe that God, who is generally considered merciful divine soul, will kill the innocent people to preserve his mystery and on the other hand incarnate on Earth to spread awareness of his existence. So it eloquently concludes the possibility of some power or extraterrestrial being who is preventing its secret from being disclosed. It can therefore be a possibility that aliens are protecting the monuments which they made with humans in ancient times. Further, it cannot be denied that most of the monuments of ancient times were made by Acoustic levitation which is impossible for us today except at a very small scale in industries. So it is a firm possibility that humans took help from paranormal powers and extraterrestrial forces to make such magnificent structures in ancient times.

We also hear instances where Gods disappeared after finishing their role on Earth and most of them chose atmospheric influences like tsunami or flood or other natural calamity to end their cycle on Earth. It is a strange fact that they disappeared in the ocean but their monuments are still preserved in the river or buried within the land. Although, many of those monuments and palaces are discovered by scientists and archaeologists but most of the secrets are still left unrevealed because the elements of nature are themselves preventing this by forcing a natural cover upon them in the form of landslides, a forestation and even soil deposits. It has been seen that the people who tried to discover the deep insights of God in kalyug, got physically impaired or couldn't survive. Today we may not believe the theory of God's curse or alien attack and may attribute health issues as reasons for sudden deaths, but the process of people disappearing in the same manner on these ancient escapes proves their factual ordinance.

There is an old theory that states that almost all of the monuments have hidden treasure inside them either in the temple doors, in the foundation or even below that. There have been countless attempts by people to fetch gold from these sources and some have succeeded but some even died in the process of finding gold. People believe that snakes and Gods themselves protect their gold and hence attack the ones who try to take the gold but the most contradictory question that challenges this belief is why God needs gold? Why the supreme owners of the universe have to guard a materialistic asset on earth? And if not Gods, but snakes are guarding treasures, then it becomes hard to believe that a couple of snakes can combat the army of gold hunters. And if we assume that an army of snakes will be present, then the present must have been visible all around the temple. So there arises a huge possibility that aliens are protecting gold and this gold besides belonging to the ancient rulers also belonged to the extraterrestrial beings. The scientific reality is that gold is used in aircrafts to control excess heat and is a good conductor, so, it can be a possibility that aliens need gold for their flying machines hence; they are protecting the same for future.

    The scientists and archaeologists have also found giant human skeletons and alien's elongated skulls buried deep inside the land and if we thoroughly study the extraordinary variety of unbelievable fossils found by scientists, we will end up in a conclusion that aliens did exist in ancient times. As the one with a human body is not God and if the human like structure had powers then it can be another well advanced species that were not the residents of earth. But today in kalyug most of us don't even know such things because we hardly invest our time in knowing the past. The quest to know the future is preventing today's human from understanding the sacred past which was certainly better than this kalyug. Many cultures not only believe the fact of aliens but also worship each planet as specific God (like Saturn which is considered the one who punishes the bad one) and they have also defined the impact of the planets on our life like in the concept astronomy where these planetary Gods are also worshipped by people to reduce their negative effects on life. This indicates that since ancient times man had a profound knowledge about the importance of universe, planets and sun, scientifically as well as spiritually.

There are many theories based on alien reality and the more we explore the more intense it becomes. Some may find alien theory totally absurd as the fear of unknown provokes them to consider every extraterrestrial being or force as God and some try to value the concept because all that we have learnt till now from gurus is still under shadow of doubts. The life in kalyug is full of stress and struggles and it is difficult for humans to explore facts beyond this materialistic life. Our ancestors may have been advanced spiritually but we are not. The theory of aliens is still taken as novel or fiction written for entertainment, read out of curiosity and the revealing of deep truths in this kalyug still needs time.

24
THE REBIRTH THEORY

We often see the stories of rebirth in movies and most of you must have read about it too. Some believe the term and some not. We cannot deny the concept of rebirth spiritually, scientifically and even logically. The reason behind this is based on both mythology and science. Mythological scriptures iterate about life after death, karma and rebirth, while science has also figured our evidences of the same. Many a times, news channels cover cases where the kids remember the happenings from a previous life and they can recall every detail from that life. Instances like these are direct indications that there exists the theory of 'Rebirth'.

Mythological scriptures state instances from sacred books or mythological books where God or Son of God, claims to be reborn and also explains the concept of rebirth or reincarnation. They state that each soul is an indestructible entity that goes through the process of birth, death and rebirth again and again. Hence, the body is destructible while the soul is not. It is also stated that the deeds from one birth are carried to the other and the calculation is maintained like books of account, which further gives rise to the concept of Karma stating that each person is rewarded according to the karma. Coming back to the topic of rebirth, it is further stated in mythological scriptures that the soul while going through various births tends to forget the previous life and in only rare circumstances do they withhold the memory. Connecting the same with the reported instances where people remember the previous life, it can be inferred that the concept of rebirth may be true.

Some mythologies explain a well developed system or concept of rebirth, taking into account the existence of spirits or ghosts, the role of fate, pain and happiness in life, the specificity of relationships explaining why a certain person is in a certain relationship with us, the predictabilities and probabilities of the next births, the concepts of Karma and its functioning, the concept of revenge, the role of God in births and rebirths and many more similar concepts which are defined with such a perfection that negating the same becomes difficult.

A spirit is born of the ultimate divine spirit, the almighty or God and starts its journey by means of a body or a vessel, coursing endlessly through Yugas until it meets the divine again. It takes and sheds the body like one changes the attire while the soul or the spirit remains unchanged. Between death and rebirth, there exists a transient phase where the spirit halts in its 'after death' form and is known as a ghost. When this phase is over, it is born anew in a new vessel, with the past memory completely erased. The life is channelled according to the deeds of the spirit and these deeds (Also known as Karma), decide everything from fate, to the transient phase to the next birth as well as the form of vessel the spirit gains. It is believed that good deeds bring fortune and good fate and a rebirth in a good family while the bad deeds bring misfortune, life of struggles and a lowly placed family. The deeds also decide if the vessel carried by the spirit will be of a human form or that of an animal. Some Mythological scriptures claim that there are 8.4 million species on the planet (which is close to the scientific estimate of 8.7million species on the planet as per the 2011 study of PLoS biology) and a soul after being reborn in these 8.4 million types of vessels, achieves the body of a human. Hence, it is stated that being born as a human is a boon and one must utilise the human birth in good deeds. The scriptures also state that everything is calculated like that in the books of accounts. Every theft, unfair confiscation of money or other similar acts carried in one birth are well paid by the offender in the other birth and that in some form or the other the spirit of the victim connects with the offender by means of relationships. Hence, it explains that the parents, siblings, spouse, children, grand children, friends, fiends and even pets connect with us to earn back their possessions. Once they are done, they leave via separation or death. The cycle goes on for millions of years in the same manner until the spirit awakens itself and merges back with the almighty.

There is another school of thought that supports the concept of 'One Birth' stating that the only birth that is known is the present birth. Otherwise too, the past births are erased from memory and future births are unknown, so by the calculation we are again left with the birth in which we are living at present, be it in any form. Since we are left with one life, it should be lived to the fullest, leaving no stone unturned and every attempt must be made to achieve everything one wants to, irrespective of methods or deeds. This also justifies the crimes, thefts, murders and escapes as well as money earned by unfair means. The births gone and the births to come will be marked with loss of memory and so the deeds do not make any difference any ways. Some thinkers also believe that we face the karma and its consequences in this one birth itself and the consequences are brought to us as ups and downs in life born as results of our decisions, while the others believe that karma does not exist and the good and bad in life are nothing but the course of life like the waves of ocean. A life of all good cannot exist, likewise a life of all bad cannot exist, but one can always escape ill fate by working smartly.

Where on one side, the concept of 'rebirth' is supported by mythological scriptures, scientific data as well as reported instances, on the other hand the concept of 'one-birth' is supported by apparent logic that negates the mythological, scientific and reported instances as well as probabilities of pasts or future and concentrates on living in the present. The concept of 'one birth' also fails to explain the existence of ghosts, spirits, paranormal activities, after birth instances, soul, spirituality and even God which makes it difficult to accept the concept of 'one birth' and easy to categorise it as an incomplete concept or a baseless argument. Either ways, the fact that one must bear the consequences of their deeds cannot be denied in both concepts and hence it marks the common link between the two concepts in Kalyug.

25
DOES KARMA WORK IN KALYUG?

Karma means action or deed, and spiritually it is said that a person gets the future according to his actions in present or past life. In other words, Karma states that the mango seeds will become a mango tree only that can never produce apples. Scientifically, The Newton's law also supports the theory of Karma as stated: Every action has equal and opposite reaction and this is apparent in all spheres of life.

Karma can be explained by simple examples: If we eat fat we will end up being obese, if we hit someone he will eventually hit us back and if we take wrong medicine we will have its side effects on the body. It is a natural and a very common concept, yet its value is not realised by humans in our daily life.

We do so many activities in our life that we are not even aware about. We do corruption to gain wealth and leisure and our activities affect millions, which we are not aware about. Suppose a person cheats his boss and makes money secretly in the purchase of product for the boss, he eventually raises the value of the product and the seller also sells the same at a higher rate to others because the employee asked the seller to make up for the extra price spent on the commodity. On a larger scale, the politicians file every commodity of less value in a ten times higher price in the tender and this over pricing is done by the private seller upon the directions by the authorities. Hence, the one who is cheated is the common man whose hard earned money is used in country's development schemes. But then the question arises 'Who will punish them for their karma?' And what will be the reaction to their action? In many cases it is impossible to catch the culprit, mostly because they escape via fine margin by building the walls of defence around them.

But we still believe the theory of karma and we are always taught that the ones who are committing bad deeds will eventually pay for it. This payback theory of Karma becomes a tried and tested fact when the culprit employees get caught and are sentenced for their cheating the company or when the politicians cease to gather votes in the elections and the opposition comes to rule. The basis of payback lies in the Karmic explanation that in one or the other form, one has to payback for his or her deeds.

But this theory is not taken seriously at the time of implementation since people develop a strong belief that they can always escape an ill fate if they cover their tracks well. And even after being well aware of this, they commit the deeds because the theory restricts people from committing bad deeds. Hence, if one would fall trap to the theory, he/she won't be able to rise up via shortcuts.

The karma theory is written in many religious scriptures and there are worldwide stories based on the theory of karma from the tales of Gods and Kings to the stories behind festivals and celebrations, the basic Karmic message that is delivered to humanity is the Victory of good over evil.

There is no human in this world who can abstain himself from lust of money and assets in his life because they form the basis of leisure, comfort and satisfaction. The value of time and spiritual self is ignored for physical and materialistic pleasures. No matter what you do, or believe in rebirth or one birth, the karmic theory applies to all spheres of life and to all beings irrespective of the religion, race, cast, creed, colour, status, language, orientation or even species. It only depends on you how you deal with it in kalyug.

26
GHOSTS AND SPIRITS IN KALYUG

A Ghost is defined as a soul of the dead person. Some are known to be seen in their previous form while some carry a shadow. Perception of a ghost basically depends on one's experience .Although every culture and religion has a different theory of ghost but there are many similarities that infer that everyone has almost similar beliefs in terms of ghosts and spirits.

Generally, an unrelated spirit or soul is considered a ghost. The soul of a deceased person who was related to us by blood is generally known as ancestral spirit or pious spirit or angel. Worshiping ancestral spirit is a common ritual done in most of the religions and various materialistic items are offered to the departed soul including food and items of utility. It is believed that the starving soul needs food and comfort. We have always been fascinated with the concept of afterlife.

Although, there is no evidence that the food or things we have offered is benefiting the spirit but most of the cultures claim that the benefit is received by the spirit either directly or through the priest who gets the prayer done for the ancestors. Many cultures have priests who also work as a medium for satisfying the soul by utilising the items or eating the feast given in the name of the ancestor. Some people also feed the animals and birds in the name of the ancestor to benefit him in his afterlife. No matter the modernisation, we do not ignore this ritual in kalyug where reality is generally ignored and constructive illusion is believed. Many gurus extend their lust to a greater level and demand expensive materialistic assets for the relief of the departed spirit and most of us even pay for the same since the fear of being haunted gets us worried.

Ancestor worship is a common ritual done by many people in their homes at the time of celebrations as well as on the death anniversary of the ancestor and it is believed that if one ignores the ceremony he will have to face bad consequences. The tell-tale turns into belief even if the ancestor coincidently appears in the dream and the fear rising from that affects so deeply that even the non-believers start believing them at some point of time. Many religions continue the cycle of ancestor worship from generation to generation without raising any doubt. It is believed that every person has an afterlife or a transient ghost phase where the spirit resides until it gets a new life. It has been seen that unsatisfied souls wander and posses people for material and physical satisfaction. The most common needs after death are known to be sexual pleasure, food and vengeance. When a spirit posses someone, we call it a ghost or even demon. They are generally called as unclean spirit since they possess the body which does not belong to them. Although, there are many known procedures like exorcism and necromancy famous for casting the spirit out of the body of the possessed but the one who is possessed is said to face the struggles later in life as well. As the body comes under possession, it becomes an open portal for other spirits as well. Although, many priests claim to be experts in physical and spiritual cleanliness but in reality only few are said to know the exact method.

Some cultures and some priests also state that what so ever health and financial issues a person faces is all because of the ghosts and demonic spirits who have secretly invaded the body and life of the person and hence the only way to get rid of financial crises and ill health is through necromancy or similar ritual. But this seems more like fraudulence than a pure real ritual since assuming everyone ill and financially challenged because of some demonic spirit looks nothing but an attempt to befool masses. We cannot ignore the fact that every person is different and leads a different life, faces challenges depending upon the lifestyle and decisions one takes in his life. A demon or a spirit may degrade the health and may create financial crises but this is known to happen only in the cases of black magic or black art. There are millions who are ill financially and/or physically but considering millions under the trap of black art seems over calculation of the rare circumstances.

In kalyug we often read about places which are considered haunted i.e. the place is under the control of some spirit or group of spirits inhabiting the place even after their death. It is said that the people who have excessive attachment or unfulfilled desire, haunt as spirits. Those who die of an accidental death, murder, suicide or similar unforeseen events, tend to remain at the place of death and often are seen doing what they used to do when they were alive. Such places have been a favourite tourist spot for atheists as well as other non believers. Their curiosity provokes them to themselves test the haunted place since the mind believes what it witnesses and rest seems like non-existent. It is also seen that the people using haunted accommodations tend to remain weak, annoyed, irritated as well as scared. The spirit may not attack them but the mere knowledge of the place being haunted creates grave fear.

Many priests even say that the size of the spirit reduces to approx a thumb size after death, i.e. about 2 to3 inches long and some even believe that they travel in a cluster of darkness. Some say that spirits wear white clothes and some have also claimed to see them in the clothes they died. Everyone has a different perception of a ghost or spirit. Some say the spirits also gain powers and experience with time while some say that they also have families.

A very confusing image of ghosts and spirits is created by television programmes now-a-days which creates an unrealistic fear in the minds of weak hearted people. The sounds and the ghost appearance is entirely a work of fiction and is meant for entertainment purpose only since a possession in a real manner is much beyond a horrifying make up and brilliant stunts. Casting an evil spirit out of a body is also not an easy task, quite contrary to all that is portrayed on screen.

Again, a well read community does not believe in ghosts and consider them fictional but they do exist and are well proved by paranormal science, experts of Extra-sensory perception as well as spiritual exorcists. The internet is flooded with information and real cases about the same. If you Google the word 'ghost' you will get more than 10 billion results showing information on the very topic and hence, despite being a topic related to orthodox beliefs, Presence of ghosts cannot be fictional in this Kalyug.

27
IS GOD A SERVICE PROVIDER?

God has always been used as a service provider by the selfish human beings. They constantly demand things from God and treat him as a service provider. Some ask for health, some ask for money and some even ask for love but God never asked any fees in return yet we offer it in the form of money, food, clothes and even other unusual things. Our desperation of treating God as a service provider is so high that we tend to divert ourselves from one God to the other if we are not satisfied by the performance of our God. Things go extreme when we even decide to change the religion we are born in, as we become completely unsatisfied with the effect of our God.

    I remember an incident, one of my friends was a serious devotee of God and he never lost a single chance to visit the temples. His father was suffering from cancer and every time he visited a temple, he would pray for the well being of his father but his father didn't live that long. When his father died, he lost all his patience and devotion and switched to a God of other religion. As he was attending the transformation programmes he said to me that I am now getting some benefits coz this new God is more powerful than my previous God. Even the spiritual dictators of the new religion mind washed him by saying that they have more scriptures that prove that their God came first on Earth. I was surprised to see his attempts and his desperation for finding the true God. The fact is, we create a big mountain of expectations and unrealistic beliefs towards God and expect him to show miracles every time on our every wish, which is impossible in this kalyug. Instead of considering God as our ultimate father we consider him as a source that will fulfil our needs.

Even after continuous changes in religious patterns and regular diversion from one God to another, the desperate humans get no relief. Many of them even take the help from the opposite side of coin and that is the help from the demons. Again, there is a huge belief in demon power and negative platforms as people believe that if God is not working for them, then his enemies may work. These attempts of worshiping evil are known to be dangerous as well as risky and most of the times they even lead to death.

The people who are migrating from God to the demon are not increasing in number but there are also plenty who create a balance between the good and bad, i.e. worshiping God as well as the demon. Again, such worships are done for the satisfaction of physical and material desires. The people, who go extreme by following demon and boycotting God completely from their life, usually involve themselves in evil or harmful activities under the persuasion of demon powers. They practise black magic and demand the fulfilment of the lost wishes and needs. But like God is unseen, likewise, the Demon seems to be unseen too, with its effect only felt.

The ultimate reality is that humans are needy and will always be, just like a human uses other human for self need, Gods are also not an exception. From positive to negative source, humans will always be hanging between the two for the satisfaction of ultimate thirst of desires.

28
WHY SOME ARE RICH AND SOME ARE POOR?

It is a thought provoking question we usually have in our mind and there have been so many reasons given in this context. Many of us believe that it is karma (action) that defines the present as well as future and sometimes we also apply this theory to our previous lives as well. A man who is born in a rich family is considered a person with good karma from his previous life and the one who is born in a slum is considered a person with bad karma from his previous life being punished with a life of poverty. All of us believe in the action and reaction theory but the argument stands undecided as to whether our life and fate are a result of our deeds or the consequences of someone else's.

We waste so much of our time in reading old scriptures, mythological tales and so many things to know the exact explanation to this phenomena but answer is hidden in our surrounding world. The most common reason for being born rich or poor is our parents, forefathers and their hard work. One generation works hard and lives a life of compromise and adjustments and the fruit of their hard work is reaped by the coming generation. Similarly, if the previous generation worked only to meet daily needs and did not achieve a lot, their successors will face similar struggles and hardships, which their forefathers had faced. What we are today is the result of our forefathers and their works.

Although, we are born empty handed with not even a thread of attire on our bodies and we die empty handed with not even a coinage to be carried along, but as we live, we live a life filled with assets and material possessions provided to and created for us by our creators, our parents. Most of the people who claim to be 'built from scratch' are not really built from scratch since for everything they know and from everything they started, the primary investment was always made by the parents into bringing up the child, into education and sometimes also training them to be equipped with certain art and today or anytime in Kalyug, nothing can be done without money.

We often envy the rich but we forget that there is a great deal of hard work coming from his previous generations, the fruit of which he is availing today and when a man questions his existence as a poor, he forgets that his physical creators were also born with struggles and challenges, and a larger portion of his daily struggles are due to the negligence of his forefathers. Some believe in a lavish life and thus work hard from the beginning. They not only work hard for their families but also teach similar arts to their successors from a very young age so that by the time the child reaches adolescence, he is trained in the art of earning. This early training provides a boost to the coming generation, their working and their financial status, quite like a relay race where the winning depends mainly on the baton carrying runner who covers the pre-set distance in a lesser time and passes the baton to the next runner much before his opponent. The next runner then, has a lot of time to reach the finish line and he can use his energy selectively without straining much. The opponent team, on the other hand, who takes longer time to cover the pre-set distance, leads to lot of strain on their next runner and a considerable amount of force, and energy needs to be invested in a lesser time to beat the score of first team. Only the exceptional runners will be able to reach the finish line in time else losing the battle is easy on hands.

But this does not mean that the fate entirely depends on parent's hard work or deeds. There are several other factors that contribute to the fate and life of a person. Relatives, friends, work mates, strangers and even the society plays a great role in the road of life. Relations, acquaintances, environment as well as opportunities affect our life positively as well as negatively in some or the other way. Some help us and support us in the journey of survival while some create hurdles, issues and hardships for us. This happens with everyone, like nature, some creatures are positively symbiotic having either mutualistic or commensalistic relationship with other creatures while some others are negatively symbiotic like in parasitic relationship where a parasite affects other species in a detrimental way. Be it catalysts or inhibitors in chemical reactions or be it synergistic or antagonistic reactions in medicines, The light of the day and darkness of the night or peaks of the mountains and bottoms of the oceans or positive or negative people or good God and bad Demon, two faces of a coin will always exist. Human and human life is no exception to the rule. You will face them both and you will live them both in Kalyug.

29
ARE WE FOLLOWING THE RIGHT PROCEDURE TO WORSHIP THE GOD?

Most of us worship God in exactly the same way. Although, the religions are different but their way of worshipping is almost same. If you carefully examine the methods of worship of different religions you will find a very common similarity i.e. offering food, clothes and money to the God. Most of us make a reflection of God in stone idols or in stone slabs enclosed in a house called as their worship home or the home of God. Different languages have different terminologies for the house of God. But a thought provoking question is: Does God really need our food, clothes and money or even house to live in? The one who is the creator of the universe, the one who is the creator of billions of planets does really need a small fragment of land entitled in his name? Does it really matter to him?

And our attempt of offering food to the one who is the guardian of the nature does really count? Does God ever ask for money? Does God ever need money to buy anything??

Has any scripture ever mentioned that God incarnated to demand food, good clothes, ornaments and money if people want to foster their wishes and needs? Don't you think that these offerings in exchange for the wishes look less like a prayer and more like a bribe?

A remarkable fact is that we really don't know how to worship God and that is a bitter reality. It is obvious that such methods of worship have been created by humans and not by God. So, it's not necessary that we are following the right way. Most of us are hesitant in donating things to servants and poor people since we believe that they have nothing to offer to us but offering to God will prove beneficial as God is the ultimate powerful entity. Don't you think that our habit of bribing people for our pending jobs is now applied to God?

Is God limited to materialistic assets? The God who is a super powerful spirit , the one who has no shape and no dimension , the one who is scattered around the whole universe , does he really need the materialistic assets for satisfaction? The one who is feeding the billions and trillions really need food from us?

n interesting fact is that we often treat the supreme soul as an ordinary soul. You must have seen the people who become possessed by the supernatural. The spirit that possesses their body uses that vessel to fulfil self needs and lost desires. The priests generally cast them out by offering tempting baits like sweets, liquors and even clothes and things have worked for many people by this attempt. It is not a myth. Science has also agreed to the presence of the ghosts and spirits.

The scientists are using various paranormal detecting

instruments today which are helping many who are possessed. There is a logic, technology as well as paranormal aspect behind this. The technology is the use of machines like EMF detector to detect the spiritual elements of nature and paranormal aspect conveys to us, the apparent presence of spirits which express their being via actions and reactions on human body. The logic that connects paranormal with materialistic offerings is the fact that the spirits are human souls that were alive in the past and after they have lost their human body sooner than their period of life, they tend to have unfulfilled materialistic desires like desire for food or even sex. They know that they cannot foster these desires without a body, so the only option they are left with is possessing a body or vessel that can fulfil their unmet needs.

We generalise the divine with the unfulfilled spirits and putting God in the same position, we believe that the divine creator also has the requirement for these materialistic things and can be pampered by offering the same because at the end of the day, God is also a spirit. The facts we tend to ignore is that the divine creator of all that exists, does not have a need or greed for any of the materialistic thing. We are not entitled to the ownership of anything we owned in our previous lives and even after death, as a spirit, we have nothing with us. There has been no record where the divine has possessed a human for these materialistic things. Even if you search the scriptures or references of paranormal cases, you might find instances where evil spirits have claimed to be angels when they possessed a body and asked for favours but none claims to be a God in need for materials or money. How can the divine be matched with ordinary souls? Can human bodies really tolerate the divine energy in them? According to scriptures, whenever the divine God incarnated on Earth, he/she took birth in his/her own human body and never possessed a vessel. So it can be said that the people who claim to be possessed by God are not possessed by God but by any clever spirit which can be devilish or virtuous. In this era of corruption and crime, God only desires humanity, the evidence of which can be seen in every sacred book.

Abundant food is wasted in temples while the masses in the world die of hunger. You must also be aware of the turnovers and monthly incomes of these religious institutions. This looks more like a business and less like devotion. If you wish to offer something to God, offer a true heart, devotion and help the needy. The divine has left these institutions of corruptions in the name of religion, long before the evolution of Kalyug.

30
WHO IS GOD?

God can be defined as a divine power which is omnipresent, omniscient, omnipotent, and omnibenevolent. He is perceived in different forms but altogether it can be said that God is an emotion in the hearts of people; an emotion of love, hope, magic, devotion, fear, and much more. They say 'Invisible like air but always present, watching over us, listening to us, shielding us and also punishing us'. He is portrayed in different forms, having different powers and also different names.

There are many theories about existence of Gods and depending upon these, people are categorised as Theists, Pantheists or Atheists.

Theists believe in the existence of one supreme soul who created them as well as the entire existence. Although, theists address him with infinite names but the divine is unanimously addressed as the Supreme Father. Many religions and cultures have portrayed God in human form as both Male and Female, considering that he has created human like himself. Some cultures also associate the image of God along with animals; some others portray God as half human and half animal while, some have long list of Gods and their families similar to human families. There are many mythological stories that express the characteristics of the supreme soul, presenting him as the best of all beings, above all evil; who shields the weak and punishes for bad deeds. To please God many worshipping rituals thus include materialistic offerings and songs of praise. Apart from Idol worship, God is also worshipped as a divine symbol. Some cultures also consider God as imageless and worship him via meditation, praying, name chanting, Holy Yagya and even by reading religious books.

Pantheists believe that the Universe is in itself the divine, the supreme God. They do not believe in a separate God. The belief is mostly philosophical and non-religious. Atheists on the other hand negate the existence of God altogether. The basis of such mind set mostly spurts from the lack of evidential proof about the existence of God and the arguments relating to it are generally based on logical, philosophical, historical and scientific views. It seen that an inability to explain the theories of previous life, karma effecting past or future lives, and many similar theories became the triggering factor for the initiation of Atheistic belief. The statements like "A child is a born Atheist and he has no idea about God." also stand as a strong fact against theism which is known to exist mainly on mythological tales and superstition.

Every religion and every culture have different explanations about the existence of God and such differences in the ideology towards the existence of the divine often becomes the main reason of conflicts, disagreements, battles and wars in Kalyug. There are many stories chanted in the name of God as his teachings from his incarnated avatars. Every story preaches a new belief, hints on a new ritual, has its own philosophy of living right and its own definition of salvation and heaven. For any two religious sects who are strong devotee of their God, it is but natural to fall into conflicts.

God is such a debatable term that almost every culture and religion has been fighting to claim the position of their god in the society and as the difference of thought is increasing, hatred and ignorance is also increasing. In all, these self proclaimed Gods create greater confusion and there comes the atheist who does not believe in the existence of God and considers that the universe and creatures are just made of some atoms and explosions.

Although, different religions portrayed their god differently, but the basis of all the religions is humanity. People have portrayed their God according to their beliefs and priorities. Besides the power and weapons displayed in the image of Gods, Colours also play an important role in the expression of the same. Almost all religions have picked a colour representing their religion just like a flag for each county. In some religious sects, the common population also prefers wearing colours according to their birth planets or generally according to the days ascribed to the deities owing to the belief that wearing a particular colour on a particular day of the week will bring them good luck.

Every religion and culture claims their God as the one

and only supreme deity. The world is hence divided into few groups of people following one particular God and claiming him/her to be the supreme most. Their beliefs are strengthened by the teachings of their ancestors who leave behind the ancient scriptures of their religion, which must be followed and implemented in life. Sometimes the difference in thoughts is so vast that God is perceived to be some extra-terrestrial force than a divine soul. But again, the perception cannot be proved until the existence and birth of God is known. Hence, the claims pertaining to God and his existence are subjective and depend mostly on one's belief.

It has been seen that people have been blind believers since ancient times and have been following what they have been taught. Sometimes the believers cross the height of superstition and perform unethical acts in the name of rituals to please their deity, for example, brutal animal sacrifices that are commonly performed as offerings of life and blood, masochistic acts by hurting the self in the name of rituals. Some religions also divinize humans or one of the couple, compelling the other to serve, worship and perform the rituals that would otherwise serve to demean their social position as a human and as an equal gender. Some others divinize the people who have traits of both male and female i.e. trans-genders and consider them as super humans or Godly souls while in some other the very position of trans-genders is that of the unwanted sect of the society. Some believers state that we are little soul parcels arising from one supreme soul and hence we all are Gods and hence advocate that God resides in all of us.

Although, every human is known to have both good traits and bad traits but the supreme divine is the perfection in its sole absolution with no evil, no negativity and is the ultimate goodness. This belief is a unanimous belief of all cultures and all religions or religious sects.

In kalyug many gurus have taken the advantage of blind belief and unreasonable fear of people and thus conned them in the name of god while some have reached the extremes of fraudulence by declaring themselves as God. The self proclaimed Gods are wide spread in kalyug, speaking at spiritual conferences where they teach rubbish to the masses.

It is also observed that people have been claiming places in the name of God and have fought brutal wars for the preservation of home for their God. This is a very common scenario and reason used to kill the innocent lives all over the world under the cloak of protecting one's religion and God. What an irony and a hilarious fact thinking that the creator of universe needs protection by the little human.

God is considered to be an ultimate source of knowledge, wisdom, humanity, life, love and the creator, regulator and destroyer of all that exists yet god is today a prisoner in temples and houses and is divided by humans. There is no answer to questions like 'How God looks like?', 'Who created God?', 'Has God created many religions or has many religions created God?' , 'Why all Gods created their human in the same way, with same colour of blood and same body system?', 'why does God choose to stay mute even at the excessive corruption, exploitation and brutality in the world?' , 'why God does not show mercy to the tormented souls or the ones who are dying of hunger and starvation?' , 'If God is not deaf then is he dead?' , 'Does he even exist?' The scriptures or mythological tales which we refer to, can be wrong as every culture and religion has their own mythological tales. So, one cannot decide who is right and who is wrong.

The people who have been an old victim of the brutality of society often exhibit their aggression and anger towards God by saying controversial statements like God does not exist or God is dead. Their patience and belief has died since their God seems to be either deaf or dead or plain unresponsive to their pain and cries for mercy and the chronic brutalities of the world has not only dried out their beliefs but also has turned them to Atheism. In fact, it would be right to call them 'Semi-theists'.

God is worshipped by almost everyone and mostly for self desires and needs. Besides worshipping, a fear factor also plays a vital role in keeping people visitors of worship houses and in staying devotees in Kalyug till eternity.

31
THE JUDGEMENT DAY

Almost every religion talks about the judgement day and it is a well believed notion passed on from generation to generation. Judgement day is basically the time of ultimate victory of good over evil by the nature or the God himself. Most of us even call the judgement day by the name of revelation or apocalypse meaning lifting of veil or disclosure of knowledge. Almost every person believes in the judgement day and especially those who have been a victim in the hands of society and are left unattended and unheard. They believe that the day will come when they will get the justice because it is only in the hands of god to omit their sufferings and issues. The end of the world is not a fascinating thing but many of us still believe that it will be a fresh start for every creature of this world including the Earth on which we have been living.

There are many dates prescribed for the apocalyptic events which will end the humanity, civilization, planet or the entire universe. The claims of the apocalyptic events have been made in history as well as in present and also for future.

The most recent date we have left behind was 21 December 2012 which was considered the end of life or the day of judgement and was a big hot topic all over the world. Although Mayans believed that this date will bring the end of the earth or the life basically by any asteroid or alien invasion or even supernova but many scientists disbelieved this myth and considered it impossible. Some even said that this is the start of the new age (Age of Aquarius) and the end of the old age (Age of Pisces) but the hope of a judgement day is still alive in many communities.

However, there are numerous future predictions as well, like prediction of apocalyptic event by Jeane Dixon(2020-2037), F. Kenton Beshore (2021), Messiah Foundation International (2026), Sir Issac Newton(2060), Adnan Oktar (2120) and many more but the people still seem less worried about these events in kalyug. Besides these predictions by experts, some scientists also believe in the theory of end of the universe but they do not generally link this with the victory of good over evil and instead consider it as the ultimate fate of the universe to end someday mainly due to many possibilities based on many theories like Big freaze, Big rip, big crunch, big bounce and many such like that.

Some even consider it pure science fiction but still there can be many possibilities of the end of the world due to many non-ignorable and uncontrollable events constructed by man and nature like nuclear war, virus spread, failure of Morden technology, fossil fuel scarcity, and environmental disasters. Many people believe that these uncontrollable events will end the human race on Earth and the reason of the end will be humans more than nature, especially because of the everyday actions of man. The greed and lust of materialism has forced humans to play with nature so the consequences are well identified which are considered a factual reality by the man of today. Many people link the judgment day with religion and everyone has their own ideology based on their religious and sacred beliefs like,

Hinduism has divided the life cycle of creatures into four periods or Yugas. Each period has its own duration of existence like this current age is considered kalyug which will lasts for 4,32,000 years [Srimad bhagvatam 12.2.1] and only after the completion of this present age the things will come to an end with a new start of course.

Islam believes in the final assessment of humanity by God or Allah. Although, there is no specified date for that but some events coming from time to time are considered an indication towards it as minor events and major events.

Buddhism believes in the appearance of maitreya basically when teachings of dharma will be forgotten and people will be more diluted into violence, corruption, poverty, illness, crimes, greed and lust. A new chapter of humanity and righteousness will be started by the maitreya.

Buddhism also believes in the theory of sermon of the seven sons. They believe that seven suns will appear in the sky causing rapid destruction of earth.

Christianity also talks about after life, second birth of Jesus, judgment day, end of the world and even resurrection of the dead.

Jewish believes in the theory of end of the days and coming of Jewish messiah, after life and even revival of the dead in their scared books.

You can go through the detail of the respective religions eschatology to know more about different beliefs and mythological theories.

The most interesting fact among all the beliefs is that they all are similar towards the concept of messianic age to some extent which refers to the state of universal harmony and brotherhood. A period of God where crime will be an extinct commodity and love and peace will be the non removable asset .Basically, a period of paradise or a period where people will be living in the God's kingdom but that world is still far away from the estimated time as everyone has different predictions related to apocalyptic event.

The difference in the time raises a doubt in many practical ideologies which forces them to consider all this a creation of science fiction and superstition. They don't feel afraid from the fact of the judgment day. In fact, most of them do opposite of the same. Instead of rectifying the negative actions before the judgment day arrival, people have started doing opposite of the same that is utilisation of materialistic assets for self satisfaction. Most of them think that after the end of the world all the leisures, comforts and enjoyments will be lost so the period left before that must be used for the satisfaction of body needs through sex and materialistic assets via any action.

I remember the time before 21 December 2012, it was a month of October and the news of the end of the world was widespread on television and radios. I was travelling somewhere and my driver suddenly asked me: Is this true sahab?" and my reaction was maybe. Suddenly seeing his over frightened yet anxious face I asked him "what will you do now?".He replied in the most calculated manner by saying that "I believe to live life at fullest, to eat whatever I want, to do whatever I feel happy in." Even his reaction was towards availing the best of the comforts he can in his salary. He was not concerned for being honest and being true as he was very near to the judgement day, but was only focused towards his unfulfilled needs and desires.

The reality is that the humans are still ignorant towards the fact of the end of the universe and are still finding out ways to be immortal. The man of today is wasting time in finding out ways to avoid and delay the apocalyptic event and is even indulged into finding the life during post apocalyptic events. In reality, the judgement day arrives in the life of every person which is nothing but the time of death. Everybody regrets the life they have availed to some extent and virtually as well as physically, everybody considers death as the judgement day, be it the death of everything that exists or the death of self and the reason behind that is the uncertainty of the future.

There are very few spiritual leaders who talk about this unlike others who are not even close to the knowledge of this unique prediction. Humans will always be confused and doubtful on this very concept and the reason of the suspicion is the illusion which is haunting every soul in the optimistic kalyug.

32
THE MAYA

The concept of Maya or illusion belongs basically to Hindu Philosophy. It states that God is the ultimate hidden reality or truth that is not easily reached by common man and the Nature (Universe and everything that is around us) is the magic or illusion or Maya that keeps the being entangled in the cycles of life. To reach God one must have correct knowledge and path that leads to the hidden truth behind the illusion or Maya.

Before we understand the concept of Maya, we must first of all understand what Reality is and what is Illusion and what is the difference between the two? If I ask you to chose between reality and illusion what will you choose and why? Most of the people answer that illusion is what pretends to exist but does not exist while reality is not someone's perception but the actuality. Some others say that illusion is something that we do not know or something that is a lie or magic or maybe a trick.

According to my observation, there are two types of realities in life. One is facultative reality or perceived reality. It is the reality you perceive or believe in, like mythological stories. A perceived reality can also be an illusion, a lie but at that point of time, it is a reality because it is being perceived, believed, lived and acted upon. It will be called an illusion only if you know that some other reality exists. Like the magic tricks... somewhere in the back of your mind you know that the sword which is slicing the throat of the volunteer is just a magic trick and reality is something else, maybe a science trick. That is our belief. But this belief in the existence of magic trick exits only when we know that some other reality is working behind the curtain which prevents the volunteer from dying. An illusion is an illusion only if we know that there is some other reality.

I will explain this with another example. Some movies show an adopted child loving his parents as his real parents until he comes to know that he is adopted. He starts searching for his real parents after the reality of his being an adopted child comes to surface. And it is only after the reality is revealed that his previous life stands as a lie, as an illusion. Before that he was living it as a reality.

The relationship of reality and illusion is like the relation of a gift with a gift box or rather a wrapped gift box. The flashy shining wrapper is the illusion and what is inside is reality. Now it depends on us. If we see, believe and live only in the beauty of the wrapper, the wrapper will be our reality. If we open the box, what we find inside is the actual reality. The concept of Maya can be best understood with this example. The Nature, Life and it's daily struggles are the shining wrappers of the gift box and inside the gift box is the ultimate divine. The one, who has the ability and knowledge to unwrap that gift box, is able to receive the gift inside. Since the Supreme divine is the rarest and the most precious gift, it is wrapped in numerous layers of the illusionary wrapper and unwrapping these layers is a herculean task in itself. And hence, it is not easy to reach the divine or attain salvation.

Maya is also portrayed as the Goddess of illusion in Hindu mythology that keeps the whole world under her spell of illusion so that just anybody cannot reach God. For this she uses five vices as her tools, getting rid of which is practically impossible for any man. These tools are: sexual indulgence, anger, pride, greed, and attachment. It can be said that while a man lives, it is almost impossible for him to get rid of all of these five vices. In the span of life at some point or the other, the man falls prey to either or all of these tools. The Nature is itself so designed that it keeps the man tangled in the quest for survival. Today it is not the question of survival; it is the question of survival with a status. It is well known that Money and Fame contribute hugely to a person's social status and the two often bring with them Greed and Pride. Either ways, to meet the daily needs of food, shelter and clothing, one must keep working and keep earning. And as the man enters the family life, he has to provide for the needs of his entire family too. The more the responsibilities he has, the more the need for money will be there; the more the frustration, the more the anger.

Then comes a time in life when we are attracted towards a person who can be our potential mate and this basic attraction gives rise to an attachment, both emotional and physical. The loop of Maya hence becomes unbreakable and the divine truth remains hidden. It takes a lot of dedication, mediation and right knowledge to decipher truth and reach God.

Whatever we believe, it creates a reality for our mind ONLY IF we know that there is no other reality to it. But then the question pops: what is the basis of concluding that the reality contained inside is a reality in true sense? Can it not be another layer of illusion? And does all the above description mean that everything is an illusion?

Let me explain with an example again. In some cultures, when the cause of chicken pox was not discovered, it was believed to be the anger of the deity and so to alleviate the effects of that disease, people started worshipping the deity known to cause chicken pox. Later, when the cause or basis of this disease was discovered, it was found that a microorganism was causing the disease and it was curable with the help of some medicines. So, everything is not an illusion. In some cases, the reality is well established while in some others it is sought for ages. Things are like wrapped gift boxes. Everything is like that in this world. The ones you unwrap, you may have the 'absolute reality' in hand. The ones you do not unwrap, you have the 'perceived reality'.

There is another aspect to reality. It is not necessary to have only one reality. Sometimes things have multiple realities to their existence which depends on the perspective. The perspective in turn makes a notion which further makes a belief. Like the surface of water in the ocean. It appears blue but is colourless. Blue is the illusion (If we go close to it) and colourless is reality. Another reality is that the surface of water appears blue since it reflects the colour of the sky. Now, both are proven facts and both are realities, but that is just not enough. Furthermore, the ocean holds a vast world inside even if on the shore it only wets our feet. When we are standing on the shore, our reality is the colourless water that only wets our feet. When we dive into the ocean, our reality is that an ocean is a whole new world with creatures never seen alike.

Now the question further arises that why does our mind believe a perceived notion to be a reality when it is clearly not? The answer to this is that when our perception is strong, the perceived notion becomes a reality with no doubts raised against it. It is only us who may or may not be able to figure out the difference between reality and illusion. Whenever the human mind wonders, it wanders and when it wanders, it discovers. But what if the human mind does not wonder? It then believes and lives the notion like a reality until it starts to wonder and question its credibility.

We perceive by way of our senses. Many people we meet, their emotions we feel and so we believe. As the awareness comes to us, we find a reality to be something other than our belief. As much we explore, as much we discover reality and we are then able to sense the difference between illusion n realities. The pitcher plant is just a fragrant plant when you look at it, the mosquito sits on it to suck the nectar and the carnivorous plant kills n eats it... reality is that the plant is death for the mosquito but the mosquito believes it is nectar of life.

Our mind is designed to be curious and to keep searching. The point at which it becomes satisfied with whatever is presented to it, it starts believing it. When it starts believing, that thing becomes a reality for our mind. This is the most common way our minds work in case of spiritual mentors who claim to have secret powers. We test their skills by asking questions related to our life or even hear success stories from people we believe in. The more our mind is satisfied, the more we start believing and that is how we proceed from being a non-believer to being a follower or devotee. The same principle works with deity worship. The prayers that come true, seem to be the tried and tested ways of worship that are sure to fetch results with a particular deity and once the notion is set as the proven fact, we start to believe in it.

In the quest for truth the question you should ask yourself is if the presented thing satisfies your belief??

Does illusion satisfy your mind's questioning and searching system? ? Does religion satisfy your mind's questioning??

Right now as you are reading, your mind is in a natural state of questioning and is searching for answers to the questions that stand doubtful to your thinking mind. In case of religion, our thinking mind is shut off in the name of scriptures, rituals and sayings in the name of God. Hence, to awaken yourself and to reach God, one must be able to decipher the hidden truth behind the Maya.

Remember that reality exists only if you realize that illusion you see is a lie and when your mind becomes dissatisfied with that illusion, only then it has a hunger to find reality. Else it believes and lives the illusion as reality.

I will tell u a joke on that and leave it on you to analyse if you are able to make out the difference between the reality and illusion.

A man on his death bed called his wife and asked "We have 4 sons, 3 well built, handsome but with the 4th one I have always had doubts that he is not mine blood. Tell me honestly if he is not my son, I am on my death bed and I shall forgive you but I shall die with the truth in my heart"

The woman replied "Honey! Only the fourth one is yours."

The man died.

33
JOURNEY OF THE SOUL

Short story by Dr. Prerna Singla.

Wandering and wandering a little girl 5 or 6 years of age suddenly reached a place unknown to her. She looked around for any sign of life, of people, of someone she may know... lost maybe she was.. and just then she saw a beautiful golden gate. All around the gate were beautiful shrubs with red fragrant flowers. Curiously she approached towards the gate and found something written on the gate in small writing that could be read only by someone reading very closely. It said "The garden of mysteries. Open at your own risk. Once you open it you'll have to cross it to reach the other side and unravel the mystery. Remember you cannot walk back."... Curiosity had the little girl exert some force and open that golden gate.

Inside she looked around, it was a mystical place that imparted an awesome feeling she couldn't describe in words. For a moment she forgot that she had lost her way. The charm of the aura seduced her into walking the sandy path with her little feet. Not for once did she move her eyes away from the eternal beauty of nature that revealed herself to the eyes of this little girl.

Walking and walking with those little footsteps she just then saw another beautiful red flower. It's magnificence forced her to extend her arm and pluck it before anyone would see. Maybe it should belong to her. She will keep it in her pocket and move on. But just then, out of nowhere a voice like a velvet hissed in her ear; "Don't pluck the flower.".. She thought to herself; "I want it.. i want to have it." .. The voice again said, "It does not matter. Don't pluck it." .. a little scared from the invisible voice the girl decides not to pluck it. Maybe someone saw her. Leaving it, with a sad face she continued walking.

A couple of steps away she saw a few birds on a branch of the tree. Their chirping felt like a beautiful melody being played in the garden. The girl was mesmerized by the melody that she heard. It made her smile again. She felt like spending the whole day listening to the chirping of birds. And just then once again an invisible voice said, "walk! .. it does not matter. Leave it and walk." ..

"I don't want to. I want to listen to the chirping birds. It is nice. "The girl murmured ... "it does not matter.. Walk!" The voice said again. Thinking of it to be someone playing a trick she thinks and then recalls the words written on the door. "You can't walk back." .. She couldn't go back. She decided to move ahead.

Maybe she cannot take anything home. The little girl had so many things going on in her mind. So many questions now popped into her little head and who was that voice?? Although it was beautiful but was overall a scary idea. And just then she saw a little rabbit running and jumping here and there. Wow!! She exclaimed. The girl ran behind the rabbit but couldn't catch up with its pace and fell off. Hurt! She tried getting up. But it ached. She looked for the rabbit but it was gone. Ohh!! She wounded her leg. Poor girl! It's bleeding. She cries. And just then the voice says again, "walk! It doesn't matter."

"Don't you see I'm hurt??? I can't even get up and you want me to walk" the little girl cried. ...out of nowhere something touched her little hand. And just then a figure seemed to appear. It was transparent as air but having substance as a human form. The girl was confused if that was born out of her mind or was it for real? An invisible lady with wrinkled hands offering help! The invisible voice had a body, a form, an existence she thought. It seemed beautiful and got the girl doubting the sanity of her mind.. "Take my hand. c'mon walk. It doesn't matter." Looking at the wound the invisible figure exclaimed.

Amazed with the beauty and grace of the old lady the little girl asked her, "Are you for real? Who are you? You're so magical. I see you like air." An expression of confusion crawled on her little face. The old lady said nothing at all. The girl said again, "I also want to be magical like you." .. the innocence of the girl made the old woman smile.. "You're magical already my dear. You're magical, in a different way. You're just not aware of your magic." Said the old woman. .. "Will you take me out of this garden?? I am lost." The girl requested.

"Sure. But for that you need to walk. Simply walk", the old woman said extending her hand towards the girl. So much of the girl's fear was gone. She thought she knew who the invisible lady was. Gladly and wanting to move out of the garden she gives her hand into the hands of the old lady. It was so soft to touch as if silk.

Soon they began to walk and talk while enjoying all the little aspects of nature around her but she asked no questions since asking question was in vain. She knew she'll get no replies. In no time she forgot the old lady had disappeared again and only her voice was accompanying the girl on that path. No matter how much the girl wanted to stay, the voice would never let her stay and ask her to keep moving.

"Why didn't you let me hear the music of birds??" little girl complained restlessly. "Listen!! Its not hear, its listen." .. the voice said correcting the girl. "It is the same thing. Just a different word." Girl replied. ... "Different it is." The voice replied.

"Okay. So why did you not let me LISTEN to the music??" girl asked stubbornly wanting the answer. "You cannot stay here all the time. Don't you have to cross the garden?" asked the voice.

The girl had no answer to the same while she knew that was no answer for her question. She thought of staying quite. After all she wanted to cross the garden.

Wondering this, the little girl kept walking. The talks made her forget the wound and pain of her leg. It was certainly a mysterious garden.

"I am tired. Let's sit somewhere." Girl told the voice.

Her little feet ached now. She wanted to settle down for some time. "No! You have to walk. Tiredness doesn't matter. Walk." The voice said the same thing all over again.

"Does none of this matter to you??? If no then what matters??", the girl argued... to this the voice softly answered " Nothing matters and everything does." ... it was certainly a mysterious garden. Everything was so mysterious.

After a few more steps the girl felt thirsty. "I am very thirsty. I want something to quench my thirst. Please!! I am thirsty." Girl requested the voice.

They stopped at once. In no time out of somewhere a pot of water appeared. The girl bent over to drink the water and got surprised to see her reflection in the water.. wrinkles all around her eyes, her face. All her body looked like an old woman. Scared she looked around searching for that mysterious voice. It was all so confusing.

The voice gestured the little girl to look back. Turning around the little girl saw, the flowers she so loved had wilted and many were replaced by new plants. The Chirping birds were long gone... the sandy path had hardened but still had the footprints of the little girl who walked that path.

Something softly touched the wound of the girl asking' "Does that pain now?? Does it matter now??"

"NO!", the girl replied realizing how she had forgotten the wound and the pain.

"Do you remember the beautiful things in the garden?? The fragrance?? The happiness you got from the music of chirping birds?? The happiness?? The pleasant feel??", asked the voice again.

"Yes!", the girl answered smiling.

"Do you want to go back??"

The girl once again looked at the path she had travelled already. Thinking for a minute she answered, "NO!".

She felt more graceful than ever, so different. Now she knew why it was the "Garden of mystery"... The mystery had finally unravelled itself... THE MYSTERY OF LIFE!!

she recalled the words of the Voice "Nothing matters and everything does..".All the while everything in her path mattered to her so much and now when her journey was complete she knew nothing of that mattered. Nothing she could carry with her till the end, all she had carried was some memories of those times.

She looked back and asked the invisible voice, "When can I see you next??"

The voice replied, .. "I'm within you. I'm the voice that stays by your side always. I'm the voice that will always ask you to keep walking no matter what. The path you just travelled is like the path of life. No matter what! Life keeps moving. You Don't have Life, You Don't Live Life, YOU ARE The Life. Whatever you do in life, you cannot walk back. Nothing stays the same forever. No one stays FOREVER including you. You have to keep moving. " And everything vanished in a blink of an eye.

The little girl found herself standing outside the Mystical Garden and now she knew she was on the other side of the park. She knew the Mystical secret now. She was changed, like never before.

www.ingramcontent.com/pod-product-compliance
Lightning Source LLC
Chambersburg PA
CBHW020853160426
43192CB00007B/903